PRENTICE HALL INTERNATIONAL

Language Teaching Methodology Series

Teacher Education
General Editor: Christopher N. Candlin

Success with
Foreign Languages

Other titles in this series include

Success with Foreign Languages

Seven who achieved it and what worked for them

EARL W. STEVICK

PRESENTED BY BRITAIN

ENGLISH LANGUAGE TEACHING

Prentice Hall

New York   London   Toronto   Sydney   Tokyo   Singapore

First published 1989 by
Prentice Hall International (UK) Ltd
66 Wood Lane End, Hemel Hempstead
Hertfordshire, HP2 4RG
A division of
Simon & Schuster International Group

Printed and bound in Great Britain at the
University Press, Cambridge

Library of Congress Cataloging-in-Publication Data

Stevick, Earl W.
    Success with foreign languages:seven who achieved it
and what worked for them/Earl W. Stevick.
    p. cm. – (Prentice-Hall International language teaching
methodology series. Teacher education)
    Bibliography: p.
    Includes index.
    ISBN 0–13–860289–1
    1. Languages, Modern–Study and teaching (Higher)
I. Title
II. Series.
PB35.S843 1989
418′.0071′1– dc20   89–8432
                                                          CIP

British Library Cataloguing in Publication Data

Stevick, Earl W.
Success with foreign languages:seven who achieved it and
what worked for them.
1. Foreign languages. Learning
I. Title
418′.007

ISBN 0–13–860289–1

---

2   3   4   5   93   92   91   90

Contents

General Editor's Preface

Teachers and learners in second/foreign language teaching and learning have come to welcome Earl Stevick's publications. What he has to say always bespeaks a lifetime of experience with learners, honestly drawn upon and cogently argued, with illustrations that have an unmistakable ring of truth. His books can be read in many ways and in many moods. Indeed, it is his particular talent to appear naive, surprised by his own data and the result of his own teaching. Such an appearance, however, is deceptive, since always his accounts have a grounding in his own work and a relevance to ours. Like many paintings, they wear their expertise and talent lightly, yet have important messages for those who would explore beyond the surface.

All this is especially true in his first book for the Prentice Hall Language Teaching Methodology series. At first glance we are introduced to a group of learners, on a stage as it were. Gradually, with Stevick's prompting, Carla and her friends tell their stories, each different yet each contributing to a coherent theme. These stories can be read as they stand, as personal accounts. Yet for the learner and for the teacher who sees them as representatives of a broader population, they can usefully be examined in the light of contemporary theories and models. This is exactly what Stevick does in his own commentaries. Notice, though, how he speaks with them and not against them, highlighting what they say and drawing out from their accounts key issues for second language teaching and learning.

Here readers with interests and expertise in second language acquisition can decide for themselves which elements from the history of each learner speak to which theories from the experiments of researchers. Matches and mismatches are equally revealing. Reflective learners and reflective teachers need to look again at the highlighted issues and not take any answers for granted, however perceptive Stevick's comments may be. So the sections on Working with Ideas invite readers to compare their own experiences with those of the gifted learners, each set of observations illuminating the other, and offering plans for action research into learning and into teaching.

In his previous books, Stevick has addressed teachers of languages. Now he turns also to learners – and to the learner within each teacher. In so doing, he provides an example – seven living examples, in fact – of how practice can contribute to theory, and how theory can illuminate practice.

Christopher N. Candlin
General Editor
Macquarie University, Sydney

Preface

'One of my students has been doing amazingly well in Norwegian. Would you like to talk with her? Maybe you can find out how she does it,' a colleague said to me one day.

'Fine,' I replied. 'How about Tuesday between ten and eleven? Maybe we can tape it.'

That conversation led me to a series of interviews with seven outstanding adult language learners. The accounts given here are based on hour-long recorded conversations I had with them. Later I conducted similar interviews with a number of other learners about whose overall ability I knew nothing. Readers are invited to become acquainted with all these people, and in this way to test and develop their own understanding of how second languages are learned. Names and a few unimportant details have been changed, but the interviewees are not fictional, and they are not composites. They are real individuals.

When I began the interviews, I was hoping to find out what the successful learners did alike. If we could teach their secrets to our students, I thought, then everyone else could become as successful as the people I had talked with. It soon became apparent, however, that learners are even more different from one another than I had expected. Success with foreign languages, I found, does not come by one simple formula. Although this fact was negative, it was useful.

But as I listened to those good learners, I also found something very positive: many of the things they were describing fitted well with one or another abstract, theoretical concept in the field. Yet they do not provide unambiguous vindication for any one model of second language acquisition. Each model will find in these interviews some confirmation, but also some challenge.

In the first seven chapters, I will first let you hear what the learners themselves actually said. Then I will provide a few comments on some of the principles illustrated, and suggest how you may work critically with the ideas, perhaps in the company of one or two friends or colleagues. There are also step-by-step descriptions of some specific techniques. The book ends with a summary of what I thought I saw these learners doing, a sketch of how I myself would probably approach a new language, and a brief statement of what these interviews have meant to me as a teacher.

As a group, these interviewees differ from many other language learners. I think, however, that the most significant lesson to be learned from them is their diversity. I assume that comparable contrasts in special abilities and individual preferences would be found among any group of language learners, no matter what their ages or occupations.

As with all self-reports, we must of course keep alert for possible self-deceptions in what these interviewees tell us. I am confident, however, that their intentions were honest, and I believe that most of what they said was accurate. As we spoke, I tried not to put words into their mouths, but only to reflect what I thought they were telling me. In editing the tapes, I have occasionally omitted material for the sake of brevity, and have felt free to reorganize or rephrase in order to improve clarity. Throughout, however, I have been careful not to change emphases or to tamper with the wording of key points.

We still must keep in mind certain limitations on such data. For one thing, in interviews of this kind we hear not what people actually did, but only what they thought they did – or what they claim they thought they did. For another, although I tried very hard not to lead the interviewees, they still may have been telling me what they thought I thought they should be saying.

These interviews are – or claim to be – accounts of experiences. Popper seemed to think that hypotheses or myths or 'conjectures,' as he liked to call them, can in principle come from almost anywhere including experience (1976). According to him, what is essential about conjectures is not their origin, but that they be stated in a way that allows for potential falsification, and then that they be tested in ways that honestly try to falsify them. McLaughlin, on the other hand, believes that 'recourse to conscious or unconscious experience is notoriously unreliable and hence cannot be a source of testable hypotheses about the learning process' (1987: 152).

Even if McLaughlin is right, however, I think such interviews can be of real and legitimate interest to students of second language learning.

- To begin with, we must remember that the interviewees' statements are in fact data – not, to be sure, data about what they did, but data about what they said they did. And these data too are to be accounted for. So, for example, Frieda's statement that memorized words became permanently available to her after she had once used them for real, but also that memorizing them ahead of time was useful, is a datum – a datum that can be explained in one (or perhaps in both) of two ways: Either she was trying to demonstrate that she had been conforming to some norm that she thought was correct, or she was reporting fairly accurately on what she in fact frequently did. In this book, I am not presenting the accounts of Frieda and the others as descriptions of 'the learning process,' but only as data – data which may possibly become sources for conjecture about learning.
- As data, these statement sometimes fit in with various theories of second language learning, and sometimes challenge them. Whenever there is an

apparent inconsistency between one of these statements and a given theory, then the theory must either show that the statement should not be taken seriously, or it must show how the statement is in fact consistent with it after all, or the theory must modify itself accordingly.

■ On a purely practical level, in the reactions of the hundred or so language teachers who have looked at and commented on these stories, I find, time and again, frequent strong identification with one or another of the interviewees.

■ Again on the practical level, the personae of the interviewees have turned out to provide convenient pegs on which my students have often been able to hang some of the more abstract ideas about second language learning.

■ And finally, becoming acquainted with these gifted learners has frequently opened my students' minds to the diversity of learning styles that they are likely to encounter in their own classes.

Other books I have written have been for language teachers only. Here, I am writing also for learners. If you are a language teacher, the experience of working through this book will make you better acquainted with the language learner in yourself. Then you will be more clearly aware of the preferences and prejudices that you bring to your work. The experience may also make some of your students' differences from you seem less strange. It may even make strangeness itself less threatening. Not least, it should give you a solid skepticism at any simple conclusions of any methodologist, including me.

If you are in the process of learning a new language, you can use this book in three ways:

1. As you read each description, ask yourself, 'How am I like this successful person? How am I different from her or him? Which of them is most like me? In what ways am I different from all of them?' Your answers to these questions will help you to understand *your own individual abilities* more fully. The better you understand your abilities, the more effectively you can use them. And of course the more effectively you use your abilities, the more easily you will learn.

2. As you work through the other parts of each section, ask yourself, 'How can I apply this principle or this technique in my own study?' Your answers will give you a better understanding of *language learning in general*. This understanding may help you to add to your natural abilities. It may also make you more patient with your fellow students. And it will help you to see why your teacher sometimes uses techniques that do not exactly fit your own style of learning.

3. After you have worked through several of the interviews, ask yourself, 'In spite of the diversity, *is there after all some pattern* that emerges from what these people are saying?' I hope you will consider that question carefully before you look at my tentative answers to it in the last chapter.

But in the end, we will not arrive at any simple formula or set of gimmicks. A few readers may find it helpful to pattern themselves after Carla or Derek or one of the other successful learners. Most of us, however, will profit best from carefully observing all of them and then drawing on our observations, the better to understand and guide our own language-learning selves or those of our students.

Earl W. Stevick
Arlington, Virginia

References

McLaughlin, Barry, *Theories of Second-Language Teaching* (Edward Arnold, 1987).
Popper, Karl, *Unended Quest* (Fontana/Collins, 1976).

Acknowledgements

This book has been made possible by generous help from many sources. Allen Weinstein, a colleague at the Foreign Service Institute of the United States Department of State, got me started on the underlying research. Another FSI colleague, Madeline Ehrman, contributed to the project in many ways. Later, Ron and Ana Maria Schwartz, on the faculty of the University of Maryland (Baltimore County), provided valuable criticism and encouragement. My students in four consecutive classes at UMBC worked through the interviews with me, and so contributed to the comments I have added. Dorothea Thorne, Donna Lewis, Max Desilets, Brian and Vicki Smith, Donna Congedo, Barbara Carter and Susan Nevins gave helpful suggestions for the last chapter. Most of all, however, I am grateful to the interviewees themselves for their cooperation, and for permission to quote anonymously from what they told me.

Chapter One

An Intuitive Learner
Ann learning Norwegian

Ann was a dignified, well-educated woman married to a fairly senior official. She had visited many parts of the world and become competent in several languages. At the time of our interview, she and her husband were studying Norwegian in preparation for a tour of duty in Oslo.

1.1 As language comes in

In the first half of her interview, Ann talked mostly about how she went about taking in new language from wherever she found it.

1.1.1 Taking language in through the ear

> ■ **Four qualities that correlate with success in academic language study (Carroll).**
>
> ■ **Starting with a clean slate (Nida).**

Hearing was clearly very important to Ann. 'I think I'm different from most people,' she said. 'They depend on seeing. I don't think I learn much through my eyes, through looking at the printed page. I seem do to most of my learning through my ears. And another thing,' she continued, 'I don't know why, but I can *reproduce* the sound.'

'You not only *hear* it in your mind, you also *make it aloud*.'

'Yes. Of course I make mistakes in Norwegian. A lot of times in Norwegian the same letter will have different sounds. Something like in English. But the printed word – I tend not to read it as if it were English. If the teacher says a letter *a* is pronounced 'ah' in one word and 'æ' in the next word, whatever she says, I try to remember it.'

'It doesn't bother you that the letters don't fit the sounds very well.'

'No. The teacher knows Norwegian. She's speaking, and I'm learning through my ear, and she's communicating, and my eye doesn't play an important part in my learning.'

'What you're talking about here is your readiness to simply take these things in, without feeling that you have to systematize them in some way? Is that the . . .'

'That's correct. And there's another thing. I consciously . . . I wash out all the other languages I know, English or Italian or German or whatever. I don't know how else to describe it. I just wash them out, and in this way I make my brain receptive for the new . . . the new stimuli.'

Comments

From time to time, students have told me that they simply cannot remember words or sentences unless they see them written down. Other students seem less dependent on the written word. Clearly Ann was a member of this second group. Here at the very beginning of the first interview we meet a theme that will run throughout this book: gifted learners are quite a diverse lot.

As Ann spoke, I recalled something written by John Carroll, who was the principal designer of the widely used Modern Language Aptitude Test. He lists four qualities that seem to him to correlate with success in academic language study:[1]

1. The ability to identify distinct sounds and to tie them to written symbols.
2. The ability to recognize the grammatical function of words.
3. The ability to learn rapidly to tie new words to their meanings.
4. The ability to identify the regularities that exist in the language we meet – to see what works and what does not.

Ann seemed to be verifying the first of Carroll's guesses. Would the other three fit Ann's experience too, I wondered?

I also remembered some advice from Eugene Nida.[2] Nida has helped thousands of people to become highly competent in hundreds of languages around the world. In his book on how to do it, Nida says that his first principle of language learning is to 'start with a clean slate.' Ann's 'washing out' her other languages was a close echo of that.

Working with the ideas

1. So far, we have learned at least four things about Ann as a learner of languages:
   - She uses her ears much more than she uses her eyes.
   - She is good at making sounds she has heard only a few times.
   - She does not mind that the spelling system of her language is irregular.
   - She does not feel that everything she learns has to fit into a clear system. Which of these characteristics do you think will help her most in learning Norwegian? How will it help her?
2. How do you compare with Ann on each of these four points?

1.1.2 *Responding to nuances of pronunciation*

> - The 'Language Acquisition Device.'
> - Data: verbal and nonverbal.
> - 'Learning' and 'acquisition.'

Ann volunteered the information that she can also mimic people's exact pronunciation very closely.

'That is to say, people who speak with different accents in English?' I asked.

'Yes, but I don't use it in a comic sense. But I can hear it. Once we were in the American Express office in Rome, and I turned to an Italian who was with me, and I said, "Do you see those two American ladies? They're from Tennessee."'

'And you turned out to be right?'

'Yes. It was something about how they pronounced the words "eight, nine, ten" when they were counting their money. And another time, at a party, I said to a woman "You must come from Florida, and your husband, he's almost from New Hampshire." And he turned white, and he said, "I'm from Lowell, Massachusetts!" Lowell, you know, is right on the New Hampshire border. I can frequently do this, though not always. But I *hear* . . .'

'You mean that you pick up these impressions of sounds from various parts of the country, sometimes consciously and sometimes not consciously . . .'

'Yes.'

'And that, once you have stored these impressions in your memory, all of this information has somehow organized itself in your mind so that . . .'

'Yes, that's right.'

'So that sometimes, though not always, you have the ability to apply that new information to new things you hear, and identify where new people are from.'

'Yes. I do that all the time.'

Comments

These days, specialists often talk about a 'Language Acquisition Device,' or 'LAD.'[3] This may sound like some special little organ, located somewhere deep within the brain. That is not what the specialists mean, however. Perhaps we can best think of this so-called 'device' as a combination of two properties of the nervous system of every normal person. The first property is that we take in and retain two kinds of data: verbal data and nonverbal data. Verbal data consist of the sounds of the language around us, and combinations of sounds, and how they do and do not occur together. Nonverbal data include other kinds of sounds, and also all the various sights and smells and tastes and feelings – whatever is going on around us. This is no small accomplishment, because those sounds and other happenings are often jumbled and incomplete. The second property is that without anyone telling us how to do so, we organize all these data that we have taken in. Even when someone tries to teach us something, the sense that we make of it may not be the sense that they intended. Yet all this somehow gets organized in – or by! – our minds. And so, within a few years, we become able to understand and then to speak. This, in a special, technical sense, is what those specialists mean by '*acquiring*' a language.[4]

Until a few years ago, people assumed that this natural ability to 'acquire' a language died out at about the age of puberty. After that, it was thought, people could gain control of new languages only by 'learning' them. In this special technical sense, 'learning' is what we do in classrooms, with a textbook, focusing on one thing at a time under the guidance of a teacher. More recently, we have begun to change that view. It is still true that small children cannot learn from textbooks, of course. But we are discovering that, to a greater or smaller extent, every adult can not only 'learn,' but also 'acquire' language.

In this sense, 'acquiring' a language means taking in sounds and experiences, and then organizing them unconsciously. If that is true, then *good* acquirers ought to be people who are particularly adept at taking in speech sounds, *and* at taking in various things from their experiences, *and* at organizing these data, all at the same time. In what she was saying about her 'ear' for sounds, Ann sounded like someone who was remarkable at least in the first of these ways. But in order to hold on to nuances of pronunciation (a kind of verbal data), connect them with where she knew people were from (one variety of nonverbal data) and then use that information with new people, she would have to be good in all three respects. That was what I was thinking about as I spoke to Ann at the end of this segment.

Working with the ideas

1. Are you sometimes able to identify where people are from by the way they talk?
   Which cities or parts of the country do you find it easiest to identify?
   What characteristics of speech help you to identify them?
2. Do you know anyone who is good at mimicking the way other people talk?
   How good a mimic are you yourself?
3. In your experience, how do people seem to react to someone who is good at mimicry?
   Why do you think they react in this way?

1.1.3 Transcribing what has been heard

> ■ The emotional side of mimicry.
>
> ■ The social side of correction.
>
> ■ The value of using one's own mental imagery.

I was interested in how Ann went about learning pronunciation.

'First of all, whenever somebody corrects me, I repeat. It doesn't bother me. In fact, I'm grateful. And if I don't get it right, I'll say it again. I keep on until I get a look of affirmation from the person.'

'But in a classroom, with other students, you can't always do that.'

'No, that's right. So what I do in Norwegian, where the spelling is irregular, I make marks on the pages of the book. If the letter *i* is pronounced [ɪ] instead of [i], I just put a little check above it. Or if a consonant letter isn't pronounced at all, I draw a circle around it. That kind of thing.'

At this point my colleague, who was listening to the conversation, came in with a question. 'I'm very curious about that,' he said. 'The textbook we use for Norwegian has a phonetic transcription for every dialog. I wonder why you developed your own system for doing this when the phonetic version of the same thing was already available to you.'

'Because then I'd have to learn another language!' was her immediate reply. 'I know there's an international phonetic alphabet, but I didn't have time, in starting to learn Norwegian, to learn that first, because that would be a third language! It would be additional!'

'From your point of view,' I interrupted, 'the marks you use are something that's part of you, and therefore they're not alien. Therefore they don't . . .'

'Yes. I don't have to learn something new in order to do that.'

'And because this system of marks comes out of you, it fits you. So it doesn't distract your eye.'

'That's right.'

Comments

William G. Moulton's 1966 guidebook for language learners contains many helpful suggestions.[5] In the chapter on sounds, he reassured his readers that most people can actually do a pretty fair job of imitating foreign sounds – *if* they try. What keeps many people from really trying, he said, is that they do not like to hear themselves sounding foreign. How can such people overcome this inhibition? Moulton advised them to pretend that they are 'making a hilariously funny imitation' of the foreign speaker. He said that the result of this approach would be a pronunciation that would delight one's hearers.

I am not sure I would give this advice to anyone. My reasons are based largely on my own experience. I am a fairly good mimic, and my pronunciation of foreign languages has always been considered very good or even near-native. Yet I have never used Moulton's trick of pretending I am making fun of someone. In all my years of dealing with students of many languages, I have never heard one say he or she had used Moulton's trick, either. My own pronunciation is at its best, in fact, when I am trying to feel myself *like* someone that I *respect*. So I was interested in Ann's remark in 1.1.2, that she never used her mimicry ability 'in a comic sense.'

Professional linguists of twenty years ago also emphasized the importance of getting native speakers to correct one's pronunciation as closely and as often as possible. Now here is Ann, a certified successful language learner, telling us that she does just that. Again, however, I think this is advice that must be handled with care. I say so for two reasons:

1. Correcting other people's pronunciation is not something that is normally done in everyday social relations. It may therefore quickly become confusing, tiring, even annoying to the speakers of the language. Anyone who asks for corrections must be sensitive to this possibility.
2. A learner who does too much of this may find it confusing, tiring, and discouraging for him or herself.

I suspect that the value Ann received from soliciting corrections came only partly from the corrections themselves. Even more helpful may have been her open, nondefensive attitude. Such an attitude would, I think, help her with all aspects of the language, not just with pronunciation.

Both her supervisor and I learned something from Ann's reaction to his question about the phonetic transcription. It reminded me of a number of experiments on the use of mental images in learning pairs of words.[6] Subjects in the experiments were asked to learn lists of pairs of words such as *flower-pen*. Later they were given one word from each pair, and were asked to come back with the other. This was a fairly hard task. It was made easier if the experimenter suggested an image, such as a flower with its stem in the cap of a fountain pen. But it was much easier still *if the subjects made up their own images*. I suspect that Ann had an intuitive awareness of this principle when she chose to 'go to the trouble' of making up her own symbols rather than accepting the ready-made ones in the book.

Working with the ideas

1. Can you think of any other reasons that might account for Ann's preferring her own phonetic marks?
2. When you hear a new name or other word, and want to remember its pronunciation, what marks or respellings do you find yourself using for the purpose?

1.1.4 Staying afloat in a 'torrent of sound'

■ **Fundamental ideas of the Natural Approach.**

As an example of 'learning through her ears,' Ann mentioned an anthropology course she had taken. 'Most people had to read the textbook over and over,' she remembered, 'but if I heard something in a lecture, afterwards I could reproduce it – though not word-for-word – and it's very easy for me to do this. I think I have an aural memory. It's the same in English or Italian or Greek: whatever the language, I can reproduce the ideas.'

'These are all languages that you understand?'

'Yes,' she replied, 'but if it's a language I don't understand, I still search. Other people – I remember once in a hotel in India where nobody happened to speak English, some people just stood there passively and waited. Not me! I was there listening. So one thing I do is, I give my full attention to what is going on.'

Did she mean full attention just to the sounds, or also to the meanings? I asked her.

'I heard a whole torrent of sound,' she replied, 'but then, for instance, when I kept hearing "Sahib this" or "Sahib that," I realized that means "Sir," and they were talking about my husband.'

'And you asked yourself, "What meanings could they possibly be associating with my husband?"'

'Mhm. Mhm. Part of it is intuition.'

Comments

Would it not be a good idea to give learners simultaneously the words and the things the words stand for? That way, the Language Acquisition Device would have both of the kinds of material it needs.

As a matter of fact, a number of methods make use of exactly this principle. Students look at carefully designed pictures, or watch the teacher perform actions, or they perform actions themselves. As they do so, they hear or repeat words and sentences that are consistent with those pictures or actions: 'This is a pencil,' 'I am going to the board, I am picking up the chalk,' 'Point to the girl with the yellow sandals,' and the like. For these methods to succeed, the teacher must be sure of two things. One is that the words themselves are clear. The other is that the point of each picture or each action is sharply defined. If the teacher controls the words and the meanings skillfully, nearly any student can follow this kind of lesson and profit from it.

But Ann is not just any student. At the hotel she is inundated by what she calls a 'torrent' of speech sounds. These are sounds that have not been planned by any teacher. At the same time, she is hit by second 'torrent': all of the actions, gestures, facial expressions, tones of voice, and so forth that are going on around her. These data illustrate no clear series of points. Unlike many learners, however, Ann does not just let herself float helplessly in these two 'torrents.' She is scanning both of them actively, and managing to pull a few useful things out of them. As a result, her LAD (see 1.1.2) is receiving data that are more numerous and more subtle than most people's would be receiving at the hotel. What is more, she actually seems to find the activity invigorating rather than overwhelming!

This experience of Ann's is an embryonic example of a widely discussed theory of adult learning called the 'Natural Approach.' According to the Natural Approach, adults acquire a language in much the same way as infants do.[7] That is to say, they acquire it through exposure to sounds of the language and, simultaneously, to the meanings that go with those sounds. During this period of exposure:

- The Language Acquisition Device sorts things out from all of the data, linguistic and nonlinguistic, that the person's mind takes in.
- This sorting-out process gives rise to 'acquired competence.'
- Insofar as he or she is 'acquiring' and not 'learning' (see 1.1.2), the adult produces language only on the basis of this acquired competence.
- There is consequently a certain silent period between the time of first exposure and the time when the acquirer begins to produce anything in the language.
- But acquired competence develops only gradually.
- At first, therefore, the acquirer's attempts in the language are just a rough approximation of how the mature speakers talk.
- As acquired competence develops over time, however, production becomes more and more consistent with the usage of the speech community as a whole.
- The acquisition process moves faster when the acquirer is free from unnecessary anxieties or distractions.
- Acquisition by adults is most efficient when they are exposed to language which they can comprehend, but which is just a little beyond what they are already able to produce.
- Learning rules or vocabulary lists, or otherwise trying to focus on just one point at a time (that is to say, 'learning') is unnecessary. It may even be counterproductive. In any case, it does not lead to acquired competence, the only source for spontaneous production of the language.

Of course Ann had not yet developed any acquired competence in the language she was hearing in the hotel. But we do see her listening silently, taking data in without anxiety, and reacting to at least one correspondence between words and the real world. The acquisition process that we outlined above had apparently begun.

Working with the ideas

1. Do you take notes at lectures? If you do, what use do you make of your notes after the lecture is finished? Do you read them silently, read them aloud, or copy them in written form? Do you discard them? What seems to be the reason for your choice in this matter?
2. If you have access to television, videotapes, or movies in a language you do not know, watch five minutes of one. If none of these is available, use a book or a newspaper. Try to give it the kind of 'active attention' that Ann is talking about. What words or longer expressions seem to have come up more than once?

1.1.5 Nonverbal communication

■ **Rhinos and zebras.**

■ **Intuition.**

'You don't just take in sounds,' I said by way of summary. 'At the same time, you're taking in what's going on along *with* the sounds – the meanings.'

'Yes. Part of it is that I intensely desire to communicate with fellow human beings. But it's not only with people. I talk to the dog at home. *And* the dog responds,' she said matter-of-factly. 'You may laugh when I tell you this, but I've talked to a zebra. I talked to him, and I taught him to do a trick. I taught him to kick with a sugar cube. I gave each of the children a sugar cube, and they kicked, and I said to the zebra, "Come on over if you want a sugar cube, but you have to kick first." He came on over and put his nose through, but I said, "No, you have to kick first." He backed off, he kicked, and then he came and got his sugar cube. Another time a rhinoceros and I had a conversation, and the children who were with me just . . . It was fantastic . . . He was responding . . . But my point is, I can communicate – animal-to-animal communication. I don't know what it is I'm telling you, but I know it exists. I can demonstrate it.'

'A kind of communication which can make *use* of language, but which doesn't basically depend on it.'

'Yes, it doesn't necessarily depend on understanding the words or the grammar of a language.'

'In that hotel in India, at the same time you were taking in the sounds of the language, through another channel you were taking in the meanings.'

'Yes. I think there's a . . . I don't know what to call it. Shall we say "psychic feedback"?'

'You mean the information – the meanings – are coming in, but you're not consciously aware of just how, or even when?'

'Something like that. Yes.'

'And you also have, at the same time, to a much greater degree than most people, the ability to . . . to get back the sounds, whether you understand them or not.'

'Yes.'

'And your mind is actively relating to both these channels at once.'

'Oh, yes! I'm an active participator!'

Comments

Ann was right! Most people I have told about the zebra and the rhinoceros have either laughed, or at least smiled skeptically.

It is true, of course, that the zebra's kick may have been just a coincidence. It may also be true that Ann's impression that she can often communicate directly with animals is just wishful thinking. At the same time, however, we should not forget that there are people who 'have a way with animals.' Some actors are much better than others at picking up the reactions of audiences. A child can usually sense a parent's mood and intentions even without words. Dogs can often do this, too. So it may be that Ann was extraordinarily sensitive at reading signals from the animals. In her experience at the hotel, the 'animals' just happened to be human. But she may also have been unusually good at giving off signals that they could read. That would account for her experiences of 'direct animal-to-animal communication.'

At the end of this segment, Ann describes herself as a 'participator.' At the end of 1.1.4, she said she makes free use of intuition. It may be that her combination of these two qualities, one of them active and the other more passive, account for much of her unusual ability with languages. Participation brings in more and better data for her LAD (see 1.1.2) to work with. Then intuition allows the LAD to work freely and creatively. All of this is consistent with the view of language learning outlined at the end of the comments on 1.1.4.

Working with the ideas

1. What is your own interpretation of Ann's experiences with the zebra and the rhinoceros? Tell the story to someone else, and compare your view with his or hers.
2. To what extent have you or people you know been able to communicate with pets without using words?

1.1.6 AILEEN: Diversity in what is triggered by intake

> ■ **Synesthesia.**
>
> ■ **Emotion as a component of a mental image.**

Ann, Bert and the others whose names head the chapters of this book were selected for interview because of their proven excellence as language learners. I also interviewed a second group of students, however. These were chosen at random, without regard to their past degree of success with languages. One member of this second group was Aileen, an Asian woman who had married an American. She had apparently mastered the language and culture of her husband's country, but I have no information about how she performed in academic language study.

Like Ann, Aileen responded to communications from animals, but in a quite different way.

'If I'm watching an animal show on TV, and the animals make a noise, I try to find some kind of pattern,' Aileen told me. 'And the same thing if somebody is talking a foreign language, I still see some kind of pattern to it. I think that's why I enjoy learning languages.'

'You *see* a pattern?'

'Oh, yes, it's like an electronic pattern you see on television.'

'Like an oscilloscope.'

'Yes. It's something I vaguely see, some kind of a wave going on,' she replied. 'Sometimes it's sort of round. That gives me the leeway to make mistakes. But if it's very clear and sharp, or very peaked when I visualize a sentence that doesn't mean anything to me, then I have to follow exactly the pattern I just saw, and that's extremely difficult.'

'With words or with other kinds of sounds?'

'Yes, like when I saw whales mating on TV, there was this noise, and if I hadn't seen that it was whales, I would probably have imagined one of those up-and-down lines.'

'If something is unfamiliar – if you don't understand it – then that's when you tend to see it.'

'Right.'

'Let me give you a new noise,' I suggested, 'and let's see how it registers.' I then said a short sentence in an African language, containing tones and some unusual consonants.

'I heard that,' Aileen reported, 'because it has a Romance pattern to it – a familiar pattern. It sounds friendly. I can tell by the tone of your voice that it's not something scornful or hurting.' She laughed. 'But the first day of the language I'm studying now,' she went on, 'there were a lot of sounds that weren't very friendly.'

'And those sounds,' I asked, 'did you see them, hear them . . .?'

'I saw them. You know, this straight line. It kept going up and down, up and down.'

Comments

The most striking thing about this fragment of Aileen's interview is her visualization of sounds as wavy lines. To me, however, two other points are more significant. One was that she reacted not to the unfamiliarity of the language in my sample sentence, but to the attitude that she read into my tone of voice. The second point is that the language she was currently studying was of a country that had had a long and sometimes unpleasant military rivalry with her own native land. Perhaps the 'unfriendly' effect of the words on her first day of class had been due more to that fact than to their phonetic structure.

Working with the ideas

1. Make a list of the languages that you have heard, whether or not they are languages that you can understand.

2. Which of these languages sound generally pleasant to you? Which sound least pleasant?

3. Can you find any relationship between their pleasantness or unpleasantness of sound, and past relationships with the countries or peoples that speak them?

1.2 The power of context

Later in our interview, Ann provided some dramatic evidence for what the presence – or the absence – of meaningful context can do.

1.2.1 What 'top-to-bottom' listening can do

■ **Overhearing a Scandinavian conversation.**

■ **The 'comprehension advantage.'**

Ann went on to tell us about a remarkable incident that had taken place during her course.

'I think it was the first or second week of class here,' she said. 'The Norwegian teacher was discussing with the Danish teacher, out in the hall, and my chair was right by the door, so I could hear. The Norwegian teacher had just given an examination to somebody who came in, who had said he was sure he would get a very high grade, when in fact he didn't do well on the translation. And they discussed this for about five minutes or so. When she came into the room, I said to the teacher, "Well, what did he get?" She looked at me and she said, "Who?" And I said, "Why, the person that you just tested." She was flabbergasted. But how did I know all those words? I don't know!'

'I suppose you just responded to all the things you did know. You put them together, and that was sufficient for you to guess. You guessed, out of all the things they might have been talking about, that this was what they were saying.'

Ann corrected me. 'It wasn't really a guess,' she said. 'I knew!'

My colleague entered the conversation. He was the supervisor of all the Scandinavian courses, and knew the situation that the two teachers had been talking about. 'This is the first time I've heard this particular anecdote,' he said, 'but there *was* a young man who came in and applied for tests in virtually all of the Scandinavian languages, and various teachers were comparing notes about it.'

'Am I remembering correctly?' Ann asked.

'You are remembering with exact accuracy,' he assured her.

Comments

The Scandinavian languages are very similar to one another. They are so similar, in fact, that native speakers of one often understand speakers of another. For that reason we are not even sure how many languages Ann overheard. The Norwegian teacher was certainly speaking Norwegian, but the Danish teacher may well have been speaking Danish – a language Ann had never been exposed to! How did she do it?

Here is where Ann and I seemed to disagree. As I saw it, Ann had two sources for recognizing at least a few fragments of this new 'torrent of words.' One source was whatever Norwegian she had picked up in her forty or fifty hours of class. The other was whatever international words may have been used in the conversation between the teachers. Ann must also have had some idea of the range of things that two language teachers might be talking about. I suggested to her that she was using these fragments in order to come up with a guess as to what they were actually saying. She, however, rejected that idea. 'I *knew!*' she said.

In a sense, Ann was right that she 'knew' what the teachers had been saying, as surely as she 'knew' what I had just said to her in English. But I still think I was right, too. What I was talking about was not *whether* she knew, but *how*. It seemed to me she was using what these days is called 'from the top down' comprehension. She was taking advantage of what she already knew about what people might want to say. Then she used the words as clues to help her decide which of those possibilities was the one that the speakers actually intended.

The approach to comprehension that we usually find in language classes is of course exactly opposite to this one. Traditionally, we get at the meaning of a word by understanding its root and its prefixes and suffixes. Similarly we understand the sentences by understanding the words, and the whole story by first understanding its sentences. We piece the meaning together 'from the bottom up.'

This incident illustrates how much more people can understand than they can say. Ann could hardly have participated effectively in the conversation between the teachers. She could not even have reported its content in her own words in that language. Some language-teaching methods have exploited this 'comprehension advantage.'

Working with the ideas

1. The techniques described in 1.2.2 and 1.2.3, below, are related to what Ann has just told us. How practical do you think these techniques would be for you personally? Why?
2. Which approach seems more suited to your way of doing things, top-to-bottom, or bottom-to-top?

1.2.2 A TECHNIQUE: Selective listening
A technique that Ann might have liked

Each of the two approaches to comprehension in this and the next section has provided its share of handy techniques. A bottom-to-top technique that anyone can use is what Nida called 'selective listening.' In this technique, one listens repeatedly to a tape recording of somebody really using the language. This sample may be a speech, or a news item, or a story or something else. Each time through, one listens for something different: the way the speaker's voice goes up and down, for example, or strange-sounding consonants, or familiar-sounding words, or certain endings that come up frequently. There are two nice things about this technique. One is that we do not worry about the meanings at all. The other is that we soak up a lot of things about the language even beyond the features we thought we were listening for.

1.2.3 A TECHNIQUE: Examining a whole newspaper
Another Ann-technique

A top-to-bottom technique that many beginning students have enjoyed uses a complete issue of a recent newspaper in the language. The learner begins by trying to guess what sort of audience the paper is published for: sensation-seekers, serious students of public affairs, a local community or some other. The next task is to try to identify the major sections of the paper: international news, sports, editorials, various types of advertisements and so forth. Only at the end of this technique does the learner look for words that appear familiar from other languages, and guess what a few individual articles may be about.

1.2.4 A contrasting case of 'top-to-bottom' listening

> ■ Overhearing a conversation in Swahili.
>
> ■ Comprehension as a generative process.
>
> ■ Varieties of components of a mental image.

I found myself wishing for a chance to let Ann demonstrate her abilities at first hand. As I was trying to think of a way to arrange something, the door opened, and the Swahili teacher came in. He said something to me in Swahili, and I replied. Ann immediately became excited.

'I *understand* it!' she cried. And again after another exchange between the teacher and me she repeated, 'I *understand* it!'

Our conversation continued for a few more turns, and the teacher left. Ann did exactly what I hoped she would: she volunteered to tell us *what* she had understood. 'OK, I can say what this conversation was about,' she said. 'His room – I'm not sure whether it's upstairs or not – his room is cold. He wants it warmer, and there's something – I guess it's the thermostat – something in the corner that isn't working.

I'm not sure what, but *something* isn't working, and you said that in ten or twelve minutes you would be able to go up – or anyway in a short period of time. Is this correct?'

'Not precisely, no,' I answered. I didn't want to break her train of thought. To my delight, she continued.

'I heard *kalienda*,' she said with some confidence. 'I'm not sure what language it was, but it sounded a bit like Spanish.'

'It was Swahili.'

'Oh! Swahili! I've never heard Swahili before. Was he cold? I thought he was cold because it sounded like the Spanish *caliente*.'

'No, it was *nakili*. *Sina nakili yangu*, "I don't have my copy." He wanted a copy of a book we'd been using.'

'Oh! I was way off!'

Comments

If Ann's guess had been right, we would all have regarded it as a brilliant demonstration of something or other. We would not, however, have been quite sure what it was a demonstration *of*. Because she was wrong, we can see some of the elements in a process that usually led her to right guesses. This process, I think, accounts for much of her success in language learning.

As she listened to our small 'torrent' of Swahili sounds, Ann was taking in and using a wide range of facts. The ones for which we have evidence in the conversation are the following:

- It was fairly cold in my office.
- The Swahili teacher pointed upward (toward the place on my shelf where the books were usually kept).
- The spot toward which he pointed was about the height at which thermostats are normally placed.
- He was reporting that something was not as it should be.
- Both Spanish *caliente* and Swahili *nakili yangu* contain the consonant sounds [k] and [l] followed by a nasal sound [n] or [ŋ], followed by a stop sound [t] or [g].
- The accented syllables of *caliente* and *-kili yangu* are the first and the third.
- The meaning of Spanish *caliente* has to do with temperature (though it means 'hot,' and not 'cold').
- My purpose in what I said to the teacher was to allow the interview with Ann to go on until the end of the hour.

So I think Ann did pretty well with what was available to her. Rather like Aileen, she was accepting whatever the incoming data triggered in her mind, and letting her mind construct images that included those data. Quite possibly Ann was responding to subtle nonverbal cues of the kinds she used at the zoo (1.1.5). With just a little more luck, or with knowledge of a few Swahili words, she might have understood us right! (And I still think this was a lot of what happened when she overheard the conversation between the two Scandinavian teachers (see 1.2.1)!)

Working with the ideas

1. Make up another interpretation of the Swahili conversation, preserving all of the elements listed in the above comments.
2. In a restaurant or large waiting room, watch people whom you cannot hear. What could you be fairly sure of about them?
   What could can you guess about them?
   What points were you curious about?

1.2.5 The need for meaningful context

■ Trouble in learning lists of isolated words.

■ The transience of 'stockpiled' linguistic material.

In spite of her broad range of strengths, Ann did have difficulty in one area. I mentioned to her that various people have different ways of learning things like vocabulary lists.

'If I ever do another vocabulary list for learning a foreign language, I think . . . well, I won't do it!' she shot back.

'That isn't how you work.'

'I absolutely refuse! I flunked Spanish at the University of X for that reason! Dr Y insisted that we learn two hundred vocabulary words a night. This was in Spanish Literature – Spanish 2.'

'Two hundred words a night. That was quite a bit.'

'Yes. Yes, it was a lot and it just overwhelmed me. So there went my Latin American Studies major! Poof! Up in smoke! And of course I was humiliated. I thought I was too dumb to learn a language.'

'Spanish was your first foreign language.'

'Yes, except for two years of high-school Latin. And I did have two years of high-school Spanish.'

'And had you had any noticeable difficulty in learning vocabulary in your other Spanish courses?'

'No, none at all. It was just the sheer drudgery. I mean, if we were *using* two hundred new words a day, and he was using them and I was using them, that would have been fine.'

'But this was just an arbitrary, irrelevant . . .'

'As if we were learning Latin or Ancient Greek, and it was just sheer memory, as if you were learning algebra.'

'Ah, so your strong reaction against the idea of ever learning another vocabulary list is only partly from this humiliating experience. Partly for you it's simply not something that comes naturally, and it's also not something that you need.'

'It's a juggling of sort of artificial symbols. But if he – or you or anyone else – were to teach me two hundred new words in *any* language today, and if we used them, then tomorrow I'd know those words! But we have to use them, meaningfully, with it on the tape recorder to refresh me at night. Then it's not a chore for me. I guess it's because the words are coming through my ears. I don't know.'

Comments

This was the first time in our conversation that Ann had shown negative feelings, in such words as 'flunked,' 'overwhelmed,' 'humiliating,' 'dumb,' 'Poof! Up in smoke!' Apparently this topic had touched a nerve! Yet in other kinds of activity, Ann seemed not to have trouble in remembering what foreign words meant. Why did she react so strongly against learning vocabulary lists?

We've already seen that Ann was amazingly good at responding to features of meaning in context. It may be that she not only responded to them, but was dependent on them. Remember the experiments on learning words with and without their corresponding nonverbal mental images (1.1.3). When one learns vocabulary lists in a foreign language, one needs some sort of meaning-image to attach to each foreign word. The only way to reach such imagery is to go by way of the native word. Perhaps for Ann the English translations by themselves failed to generate nonverbal images that were vivid enough and complex enough to enable her to hold on to the Spanish words.

It was as though Ann's Spanish professor had asked her to lay in a supply of food or water, one potato or one bucketful at a time, for a long trip that she might take at some unspecified time in the future. This is what we will hear Frieda refer to as 'stockpiling' (6.2.3). There are five things to remember about stockpiling of purely linguistic material – words, grammatical structures or just plain sounds – with no attached meanings:

- As we will see in the other interviews, people differ somewhat with regard to their ability to stockpile linguistic material.
- At best, though, the shelf life of unattached linguistic material is rather short.
- People differ also in their willingness to stockpile. After all, if the potatoes are going to spoil or the water is going to evaporate before we have a chance to take advantage of them, why go to all the effort of accumulating them in the first place?
- Even so, some people can make significant use of stockpiling. (You may or may not be one of these people.)
- The only real way to be sure the supplies do not go bad or disappear is to eat them or drink them – to work them into real use of the language – just as soon as possible. (This is what Ann was talking about when she said, 'If we had used the words, I'd know them!')

Working with the ideas

1. If you had to learn twenty foreign words with their equivalents in your native language, for a test tomorrow, how would you go about it?
2. Learning isolated vocabulary is apparently Ann's least favorite aspect of language study. What is yours?

1.2.6 Ann's idea of the 'natural' way to learn a language

> ■ Side effects of assuming that all language students are basically like oneself.
>
> ■ Omaggio's list of qualities of successful language learners.

As our conversation drew to an end, Ann remarked, 'Every child who has learned to speak before the age of five has learned in the same way we . . . the way I learned English or any language, and it has been the method I've been using to learn Norwegian now!'

'You feel that what you're doing is very much *like* the way you learned English.'

'Yes. And that using the written material in the course is superimposed – culturally superimposed. I want to say that we're using another tool, and using our eyes as a training aid.'

'But the basis of it is this same way you learned English?'

'Yes.'

'You seem to be saying that if you had to depend on what's in this book, without having available the way you learned English, then you'd be in trouble.'

'For me, without a native speaker . . .'

'What I mean is, if you didn't have available to you the same mechanism that you used for learning English . . . if you *had* to depend entirely on this book or some other book, then you might find it much more difficult.'

'It would be like learning to speak algebra. It would be like learning those two hundred words in Spanish. Apparently I can't . . .'

'Abstract? Dead?'

'Yes! Both! Absolutely!'

Comments

Ann seemed to attribute her success in language learning to just conforming to a natural process. She evidently believed that what was natural for her was natural for everyone. This belief has played three roles in the history of the learning and teaching of languages. First, it has encouraged teachers to devise methods based on their own learning and that of their best students. Second, it accounts for much of the disappointment experienced by these same teachers, or by others who adopt their methods, when the methods fail to work with all students. Finally, it has left many unsuccessful students feeling that something is wrong with them. For some of those students, at least, their nature was simply different from what the deviser of the method had assumed it was.

We can now compare what we know of Ann with Carroll's list (1.1.1). We have already seen that she is good at identifying sounds and attaching them to symbols. (She even prefers to make up her own symbols!) As with *sahib* in the Indian hotel, she finds it easy to tie new words to their meanings (provided they are in context). In fact (as with the Swahili conversation), she sometimes comes up with more meanings than she needs! But this interview has told us nothing about her abilities to identify grammatical functions of words, or to see what is or is not done in putting sentences together.

More recently, Alice Omaggio has provided a somewhat different list.[8] It contains seven characteristics of successful language learners:

- *They have insight into their own learning styles and preferences.* Ann certainly has!
- *They take an active approach to the learning task.* Ann certainly does!
- *They are willing to take risks.* We have seen that Ann is.
- *They are good guessers.* Ann is a champion in this respect!
- *They watch not only what words and sentences mean, but also how they are put together.* Ann didn't say much about this. I suspect she is fairly good at it, however.
- *They make the new language into a separate system, and try to think in it as soon as possible.* This was one of the first things Ann told us about herself.
- *They are tolerant and outgoing in their approach to the new language.* Apparently Ann is.

So the interview with Ann supports my hunch that all of the items on Omaggio's list contribute toward success in language learning. If I had interviewed only Ann, I might have concluded that every good learner is like her. I was to find out very soon, however, that such a conclusion would have been wrong.

Working with the ideas

1. What overall differences do you notice between Carroll's list and Omaggio's list?
2. Look through the interview once more and pick out the evidence to support the idea that Ann fits Omaggio's criteria.
3. Which of Omaggio's criteria fit you most closely? Which fit you least closely?

1.3 Notes

1. John Carroll's list appears in 'Twenty-five years of research on foreign language aptitude,' a chapter in *Universals in Language Learning Aptitude*, edited by Karl C. Diller (Newbury House, 1981).
2. The revised edition of Eugene Nida's book *Learning a Foreign Language* was published by the Friendship Press in New York City, in 1957.
3. There are numerous treatments of the 'LAD' concept as it applies to language learning. Heidi Dulay, Marina Burt and Stephen D. Krashen mention it in their book *Language Two*, which was published by Oxford University Press in 1982. In the second edition of his *Principles of Language Teaching and Learning* (Prentice Hall International, 1987), H. Douglas Brown gives a brief critical discussion of it.
4. The distinction between 'acquisition' and 'learning' is a conspicuous element in all of the works of Stephen D. Krashen, including the one cited in the preceding note.
5. William G. Moulton's very readable book, titled *A Linguistic Guide to Language Learning*, was published by the Modern Language Association in 1966.
6. The research to which I am referring here was reported in the *Journal of Mental Imagery* by M. J. Dickel and S. Slak, in an article titled 'Imagery vividness and memory for verbal material' (1983, vol. 7.1).
7. *The Natural Approach* is the title of a book by Stephen D. Krashen and Tracy Terrell, published by Prentice Hall International, 1983.
8. This brief report by Alice Omaggio, titled 'Successful language learners: What do we know about them?,' appeared in the ERIC/CLL News Bulletin for May 1978.

Chapter Two

A Formal Learner
Bert learning Chinese

Another very successful language learner was Bert, a young diplomat who had reached an extraordinarily high level of competence both in speaking and in reading Chinese. At the time I talked with him, Bert was studying another Asian language.

2.1 Audio-Lingual-style activities

Many of the techniques that Bert told me about were typical of the well-known Audio-Lingual method.

2.1.1 Bert's idea of the 'natural' way to learn a language

> ■ **Grammar–Translation.**
>
> ■ **Audio-Lingualism.**

'I suppose like most people I have firm ideas which aren't shared by everybody,' Bert began, 'but what seems to work for me is simply the approach which I suppose is just to imagine you're a baby or an infant learning a language again. You begin by listening, listening, listening, absorbing, repeating to yourself, repeating after the teacher, making certain that you understand the vocabulary, and then using it, preferably in simple sentences, and then building up from there.'

'In the beginning, the teacher would say a word or a sentence, and you'd repeat after her.'

'Or him. Yes, that's right.'

I remembered that Ann had ended her interview with the remark about learning Norwegian the way she had learned English. Now Bert was beginning with that same assertion. His description so far did not sound entirely like the children I had observed or read about, but I did not want to distract him. 'Like a baby,' I repeated.

'Yes, the so-called natural approach to learning,' Bert replied. 'In high school I had Latin, French and Russian, and I learned them all in the traditional way, which is to say the grammar way.'

'Where you sit down and read about it.'

'Well, you sit down and read it, and you decline and you conjugate. And what I found from that was that I could *read* Russian quite well, but I was never particularly good at speaking Russian. Similarly with French and also of course with Latin.'

Comments

In order to understand what Bert is talking about in this interview, we need to look first at two contrasting approaches to the learning and teaching of foreign languages. These are Grammar–Translation and Audio-Lingualism.

Grammar–Translation was the most widely accepted approach during the period before the end of World War II.[1] Bert's description of it is only partial. A typical lesson began with a list of words in the language to be learned, together with native-language equivalents. Then came a number of grammatical rules with illustrations. There might or might not be a brief reading which contained examples of the new words and rules in context. Finally, there were sentences to be translated from the foreign language to the native language, and others to be translated from the native language to the foreign language. The book also contained paradigms – tables showing all the forms for sample nouns, adjectives and verbs of various kinds. Students were required to memorize the paradigms well enough so that they could recite them aloud or reproduce them on paper. Knowledge of paradigms enabled the student to avoid errors in translation into or out of the foreign language. If there were other ways to correctness, this method did not know of them.

The social setting of Grammar–Translation is worth a brief look. It flourished during a period when higher education was much less widespread than today. The students, or at least their teachers, had grown up in a world where only a minority even completed secondary school. International travel and access to mass media in other languages were relatively rare. Given the students and teachers in foreign-language programs, translation seemed the only common objective available.

In the late 1950s and the 1960s Grammar–Translation was challenged and partially replaced by a new approach, which eventually received the name 'Audio-Lingual.' Audio-Lingualism emphasized learning to speak and understand the new language.[2] Reading and writing, when they were taught, were built on these oral skills. Language was primarily *speech*, and its use was controlled by *habits*. Habits were manifested by the use of the speech *muscles*, and so they could only be formed through active use of those muscles in oral *practice*. Practice was to be repeated as often as necessary in order to ensure *accuracy*. Only after accuracy was established should any learner attempt *fluency*.

The Audio-Lingual approach gave rise to a number of methods. In the best-known of these, a typical lesson began with a dialog. Students repeated the dialog after their teacher, who corrected their pronunciation as necessary. They then continued practice on the dialog until they could recite it rapidly and accurately from memory. Only after they had done so did they meet a series of notes explaining grammatical features that had been exemplified in the dialog. The way to accurate control of grammar was not through memorizing paradigms, but through performance of drills. A drill consisted of a series of sentences which the student was to give in response to a series of cues. A simple English example, designed to teach the present-tense forms of the verb *be*, is as follows:

Cue	Expected response
	I am busy.
she	She is busy.
we	We are busy.
	etc.

The lesson might end with extra listening practice, recombining material from the basic dialog and the exercises, or with speaking activities, or in some other way.

The social setting of Audio-Lingualism is also interesting. World War II suddenly placed two new demands on language teaching in the United States. One was for face-to-face communication skills. The other was for instruction in dozens of languages from all over the world – languages for which no lesson materials existed. Responsibility for this training was given to a group of anthropological linguists. Not being language teachers, the linguists were unattached to the classical and liberal assumptions of traditional language-teaching. Instead, they tended to be behaviorists, anti-mentalists and very pragmatic.

This team trained hundreds of service personnel in languages from Albanian to Zulu. Though their success was not as uniform as journalists made it sound, it was a truly noteworthy accomplishment. The result was enormous prestige and substantial public support for the linguists and for the methods they had used.

World War II was won by troops who had become convinced of the value of calisthenics, military drill, unquestioning acceptance of authority and 'sounding off' in a loud, firm voice. All of these features appeared in Audio-Lingualism. The military life also demands spartan willingness to put up with temporary discomfort for the sake of future objectives. This quality was required, for most people at least, in order to endure four features of Audio-Lingual courses. One of those features was the massive repetition of dialogs and drills. Another was the memorization of long dialogs. Still another was the belief that seeing the written materials prematurely would keep students from hearing the nuances of sounds. The fourth was expressed in the admonition 'Say it this way because the native speakers say it this way. Don't ask why!'

Beginning in the late 1960s, other approaches have challenged and largely replaced Audio-Lingualism in many parts of the world. We do not need to understand them, however, in order to follow what Bert is going to tell us in the remaining segments of this interview.

Working with the ideas

1. Bert recites a series of activities in which he says babies engage when they are learning their first language. Which of these fit your observation of babies you have known? Which do not?

2. In this segment and in those that follow it, what references can you find to the principles of Grammar–Translation and Audio-Lingualism?

2.1.2 Massive 'mimicry-memorization'

> ■ **Connecting meanings and sounds.**
>
> ■ **Concentrating on meanings or sounds.**

'So the first experience I had in going at it in any other way was with Chinese, where the director insisted that we adhere to his special method. It was a controversial method, in which I happen to be a true believer.'

'You found it quite effective.'

'I certainly did! His method was, very simply, repetition, repetition, repetition, starting with very basic sentences, and an absolute prohibition on the use of English at any time in the class. Further, and I suppose this was the most controversial point, there was an absolute ban on bringing any written materials at all into class.'

'There were three ways in which it differed from your Latin, French and Russian: the constant physical repetition, the complete monolingual atmosphere, and also the fact that you didn't work with written materials at all.'

'Yeah, I'd say that for the first six months, six hours a day, it was entirely one-on-one, entirely in Chinese, entirely either repeating after the teacher, or attempting to construct simple sentences . . .'

'This was your very first contact with Chinese?'

'No, actually, I'd had a year of Chinese in college. But now it was just repetition, construction of simple sentences and constant correction.'

'Correction by the teacher.'

'By the teacher, yes. And in that program, one of the teachers had special responsibility for correcting pronunciation. Other teachers would concentrate on other aspects.'

'Such as grammar?'

'No, not grammar. Actually, during the first six months there was no discussion of grammar *per se*. In fairness, though, Chinese is easy as far as grammar is concerned.'

'But in any case, it was pretty much *doing* the language, not talking about it.'

'Yeah. If we had any questions about grammar, we could go home and look it up in a textbook. But we couldn't ask the teacher about grammar, even in class.'

Comments

Bert says that Chinese is easy as far as grammar is concerned. By this he means that it does not have large sets of endings for its nouns, or irregular verbs, such as he had found in Latin, French and Russian.

'Nobody can learn a language from all that parroting!' a colleague of mine once fumed. She was criticizing the then-new Audio-Lingual approach (see 2.1.1). She would have said the same about the first few months of Bert's Chinese course.

Any language deals with two realms. One is the realm of meanings: messages that we want to convey. These messages contain components of many kinds: descriptions, locations, narratives, of course, but also emotions, purposes and personal relationships. The other realm consists of speech sounds, written symbols and, for some people, sign language. A language is just a system for relating these two realms to one another.

My colleague might also have pointed out that Bert was not only learning a new language; he was also learning a new culture. Learning Chinese culture meant becoming familiar with the range of meanings that other people might want to convey, some of which were different from the meanings Bert was used to at home. It also meant learning how those meanings fit together in the lives of Chinese people.

Eventually, if he was to succeed, Bert (like any other learner) had to have two kinds of things in his head at the same time. He had to have some sounds or written symbols. Alongside them, *at the same time*, he also needed to have some meanings that corresponded to those sounds. But the meanings we have in our heads at any moment may be pale and impoverished, or they may be vivid and complex. My colleague was saying that in massive repetition and correction – 'parroting,' as she called it – Bert was concentrating on the first of those two realms at the expense of the second. He was learning to manipulate the forms, but not to relate the forms to meanings. This was the kind of thing that had made Ann so uncomfortable in her study of Spanish vocabulary (see 1.2.5, 1.2.6). And yet we know that Bert did learn Chinese extremely well.

Working with the ideas

1. How successful do you think this kind of course would have been for you?
2. How do you think you would have reacted emotionally to it?
3. Which features of it would you have found most acceptable? Why? Which least acceptable? Why?

2.1.3 Intensive mechanical drill

> ■ **Reading authentic materials.**
>
> ■ **Patterns.**
>
> ■ **'Burning patterns into the brain.'**

Bert continued. 'For face-to-face purposes, and understanding contemporary press, radio, that sort of thing, I found this method just about ideal.'

'So the sentences you used in this study were sentences you knew the meaning of, whether because there was an English translation, or because the teacher demonstrated the meaning.'

'Yes, both. Sometimes one and sometimes the other.'

'Nevertheless, in class you left the English aside, and that was the big feature as you perceived it.'

'Yes, all new vocabulary was explained in Chinese – learning it as a native would learn it, more or less. Then in the later stages, with college textbooks and the like, we had to do a lot of preparation outside of class. A lot of dictionary work, and then come in and recapitulate in class what had been read the preceding night. This was basically an hour a day throughout the course. At other hours, we'd do other things, such as culture.'

'Again in Chinese.'

'Oh, yes, in Chinese.'

'And in the progression from first-grade texts to college texts and radio plays, and hearing about Chinese culture in Chinese, there was a certain authenticity there. An authenticity that made it easier when you went out of the school to talk to people. You didn't run into any discontinuity or barrier or anything.'

'Right. Right.'

'You were very quickly getting into genuine use of Chinese, based on what you had studied in a very mechanical way.'

'Yes, and that was quite different from what's going on in the language I'm studying now. Here they turn everything into translation practice, even drills that I'm fairly sure the author didn't intend to be used that way. I think all of us have been feeling that we need more interaction with the language.'

'Interaction with the language, whether through meaningful conversation, or just through repetition . . .'

'Exactly! In other words, something that will burn the patterns into our brains!'

Comments

As Bert reads authentic materials written by and for Chinese people, he is not only picking up how the purely linguistic elements fit together; he is also finding out what meanings exist in Chinese life that do not exist in his native culture, and how some of these meanings are connected to one another.

Bert reacts quite differently to translation than he did to paraphrase. One part of the reason for his preference is certainly that in paraphrasing, the original was in Chinese. Perhaps another part of the reason is that in paraphrase he had to first form in his mind a nonverbal image of the meaning of the original. Then in making his Chinese paraphrase, he had to draw on that imagery, just as in normal speaking we try to express meaning-images that we have in our minds. In translation, on the other hand, he was working from a set of English words.

To me, the most interesting part of this segment is Bert's last statement. In 2.1.1, we saw an English example of what Bert means by a 'pattern': we automatically use *am* after *I*, *is* after *he*, *she*, *it*, and *are* after *we*, *you*, *they*. 'Burning patterns into brains' is a concept typical of Audio-Lingual thinking, though it did not originate there. This kind of activity concentrates on the realm of language form, with little or no attention to the realm of meaning. It is really a kind of 'stockpiling,' like what we saw in 1.2.5. There are two obvious differences:

■ What Bert is stockpiling is grammatical reflexes, while Ann was trying to stockpile vocabulary.
■ Bert seems quite content with doing such things; Ann clearly was not.

The 'burning' metaphor probably comes from the branding of cattle, a process which causes temporary pain but produces permanent results. In language study it refers to the performance of many dozens, even hundreds of repetitions, either oral or written. In deciding whether to study in this way, one must compare the pain (tedium, fatigue, frustration, wondering 'Is it worth it?') against the result (improved control of some feature of the language). For some learners the balance will go in one direction, while for others it will go in the other.

Working with the ideas

1. Suppose you received an important document whose number was A9035591-D. How would you go about memorizing the number so that you could be sure of being able to produce it accurately when needed?
2. How have you reacted (or how do you think you would react) to being put through the same oral drill ten times without stopping?

2.1.4 How important is native-like pronunciation?

■ **Meaning-bearing differences in sound vs nuances.**

■ **Social and personal significance of nuances.**

'What about your pronunciation?' I asked.

'It's lousy!' Bert confessed. 'In any language I speak, I'll speak with a Chicago accent, I have no doubt. By and large I seem to be able to reproduce *sounds* with no difficulty. But intonation gives me a great deal of difficulty.'

For me, the word 'intonation' has to do with the way the pitch of the voice rises and falls. In Chinese, two words with quite different meanings may have the same vowels and consonants, but differ only in the pitch pattern that they carry. So I asked, 'Such as the tones in Chinese?'

'Tones, no. I can reproduce the tones in Chinese. That's no problem. If you give me a single character, I can give you the pronunciation and the tone. But putting it together in a long sentence, inevitably I'm going to come out with a foreign intonation. No question about it. My pronunciation was rated as something that can be understood easily enough, but that's still noticeably foreign in intonation.'

I concluded that Bert was talking about what most people call a 'foreign accent.'

'As I think back, no one ever corrected this,' Bert recalled. 'It was enough for our teachers if we got the sounds and the tone of a word correct. Which I think is fair enough. After all, my face is white and my eyes are round and my nose is big. So I'll never be mistaken for a Chinese. My objective was simply to be understood easily.'

'You don't see yourself as much of a mimic in foreign languages?'

'No, I don't. No.'

Comments

Why do some people develop excellent pronunciation in foreign languages, while others retain a strong accent? No one knows for sure. One guess is that it is something like musical ability. A few people seem to have been born 'tone-deaf,' while a few others naturally have the ability to acquire 'perfect pitch.' Maybe the ability to pick up accents is innate in the same way.

Another guess is that the difference is due to the meaning of accents. Children as they grow up tend to copy very closely the pronunciation of those around them. But small differences in pronunciation are used in two ways. One is to tell words apart: the difference between English *deed* and *did*, for example. In many other languages this same difference in sound never makes a difference in meaning. Speakers of those languages tend to confuse *deed* with *did*, or *eat* with *it*, when they use English. Bert's Chinese must have been pretty good in this respect: 'My pronunciation was rated as something that can be understood easily enough'; and 'If you give me a written character, I can give you the pronunciation and the tone.'

In the same way, speakers of English have trouble hearing and producing the difference between French *vous* 'you' and *vue* 'vision.' They tend to use the same vowel that they use for their native English pronunciation of *two*. For most English speakers, that sound is closer to the one in French *vous*. For others, however, their vowel in *two* is closer to French *vue*. Both vowel sounds exist in English, then; which one you use depends not on what you mean, but on where you are from. And this is the second use of small differences in pronunciation: to show which group you belong to, geographically and socially.

A 'foreign accent' consists of many small differences of pronunciation. Some of these differences are of the first kind – the kind that serve to distinguish words of different meanings. Most of them, however, are of the second kind – the kind that indicate identification with one or another group. In this view, people's ability or inability to acquire a 'good accent' may actually say something about their willingness or unwillingness to sound like someone outside their home group. Bert's remark is of interest here. He didn't mind not having been taught an accurate accent in Chinese: 'After all, my face is white and my eyes are round and my nose is big. So I'll never be mistaken for a Chinese.' This is quite different from what we will hear Ed (see 5.1.3), Frieda (see 6.3.4) and Gwen (see 7.2.2) saying later on.

Working with the ideas

1. If you have ever studied a foreign language, what are some of the new sound distinctions that you had to learn in order to keep different words from sounding the same?
2. Within your native language, which other geographical or social groups would you be most comfortable sounding like? Which least comfortable?

2.1.5 Memorization of texts

> ■ **'Learning' and 'acquisition' again.**
>
> ■ **Problems with mixing social levels in beginning materials.**

'What about memorizing connected texts in a foreign language, such as dialogs or little stories or the like?' I asked. 'Is that something you thrive on, something you can do but don't care for, something you detest?'

'Well, this is essentially what we were required to do in Chinese. Within reason, of course. I mean, one doesn't sit down and memorize three pages of text – of narrative, but there is something to be . . .'

'Memorization wasn't something that particularly bothered you?'

'No. No, within reason. By that I mean that one had to have assurance that this was what people really said. If I was going to spend the time on it, I wanted to be sure it was going to be worth the effort.'

'But memorizing twenty or twenty-five lines, or something like that . . .'

'No, that didn't bother me.'

'You'd go home and do it, and bring it back the next day, and . . .'

'Yes, and I stress that because, with the text we're now using in this language, I think all of us have a feeling that the language in the book is rather stilted and artificial, and not necessarily what we'd be saying.'

'That feature of the Chinese course was what gave you an instinct for what is actually said in the language – for how sentences are put together.'

'Yes. In this language I feel that I just have countless patterns sort of swimming around in my head.'

Comments

Bert is complaining that in his present course, samples of language appropriate for one situation or one social level are mixed with samples appropriate for other situations and levels. This causes trouble whether he is 'learning' or 'acquiring' the language. (In Chinese he seems to have done some of both.) 'Learning,' in the narrow sense described in 1.1.2, is something like playing an intellectual game. To ask a learner to keep track of new patterns on more than one social or geographical level is like asking a new checkers player to play on a three-dimensional board. 'Acquisition' is more like developing a new self, and the same complications can keep that self from developing in a well-integrated way. To use yet another figure of speech, Bert must have felt like a beginning marksman who is asked to shoot at a moving target before he has learned to hit a stationary one.

Working with the ideas

1. Which variety of language would you prefer to meet first as a learner?
2. Examine a textbook for teaching your language to speakers of other languages. What variety or varieties of the language does it teach? Colloquial? Formal? Spoken? Written?

2.2 Bert's other activities

Others of the things Bert told me about were not clearly derived from the techniques that are standard in Audio-Lingual language study.

2.2.1 Memorizing individual words

- **Vocabulary cards.**

- **The importance of personality type (Myers–Briggs test, etc.).**

'Anything in the general area of learning vocabulary?' I inquired. 'Some people use word cards, and some people do other things.'

'I've done it both ways. Really, I swore off cards.' Bert paused. 'I have a trick memory,' he went on. 'That's probably the thing I'm best at in language learning. I do tend to remember words for everything. So in the past I never did cards. This time, I thought I'd do it. When I make cards now, I make a card *with* the word, but I always do a full sentence, and then attempt to know the word *in* the sentence. I think making cards with a vocabulary word and then a corresponding word in English is a waste of time because you don't know how it's used.'

'Then what you do is put the foreign language sentence on one side . . .'

'What I do is put the foreign word on one side, and a whole sentence using the word on the other side.'

'Aha! Then the whole card is in the foreign language!'

'As I said, I think my trick memory was what let me get a perfect score on the aptitude test.'

'A memory that lets you get things back mostly visually?'

'Yes, it's primarily visual. In Chinese I could give you the shape of the written character along with the pronunciation and the tone. If you give me a list of things, I can memorize them somewhat more rapidly than most other people.'

'That must be very handy!'

'Well, yes, but it doesn't at all mean I'm going to be able to put them into a nice fluent sentence. But in Russian and French it kept me from having to study at home.'

'You didn't necessarily write it down. You just heard the word used in discourse, or you heard that this Russian word means this English word, or . . .'

'Yes, both ways. Back when I was a kid I could memorize baseball averages very easily, too. That kind of thing. Not particularly admirable. It's just there.'

'But you do find, though, that if you get into the middle of a sentence in a foreign language, and you want to say something, that you can sort of turn on this memory and pick out the word you need? Or doesn't it work that way?'

'If language were only a series of vocabulary words strung together, I'd do fine!'

Comments

In making his flashcards, Bert makes no use at all of his native language. He simply relates a word in the foreign language to a sentence in the same language. That way he avoids interference from English. (Of course, that sentence must be one that he can largely understand, so that it provides context for the word.)

Both Bert and Ann had something to say about the learning of vocabulary lists. But where Ann despaired of it, Bert has a special gift for it. We will meet many more examples of just how different outstanding learners are from one another.

Some scholars have investigated relationships that exist between differences of psychological type, and differences in how people learn languages. One such study concluded that:

> *the current approach* [my italics] to presenting material and structuring learning is better suited in general to learners (a) who are able to work alone efficiently, to concentrate well, and avoid outside distractions (Introverted); (b) who tend to be global learners, have a natural flair for abstract thinking and have a tolerance for theory (Intuitive); and (c) who like to live life in a planned, orderly, and organized way (Judging).'[3]

(The terms Introverted, Intuitive and Judging are used here as they are in the Myers–Briggs Type-Indicator studies.)

Working with the ideas

1. Bert remarks that language learning is more than just learning words. List some other knowledge and skills that are required in order to control a new language. (Your list may come from your experiences as a language learner, or from the comments on the preceding sections of this book.)
2. Carroll (see 1.1.1) and Omaggio (see 1.2.6) have provided lists of characteristics of successful language learners. Review Bert's interview with those lists before you.
   In what ways is Bert's description of himself consistent with those lists? In what ways is it inconsistent? Support your answers with quotations from the interview.
3. How would you guess Bert and Ann compare with regard to the description given at the end of the comments for this section, based on the Myers–Briggs Type-Indicator? What possible links do you see between these traits and the ways in which these two people went at language?

2.2.2 A TECHNIQUE: Imagery with vocabulary cards
A technique from Bert

In my own study of other languages I have used two variants of Bert's technique. One is to replace the word by a blank on the sentence side of the card. Then I can start by looking at either side, and test myself by trying to give the other. A second variant is to put the word on one side and some crude pictorial representation of its meaning on the other. I'm very poor at drawing, but the fact that I'm the only one to use the cards makes artistic quality irrelevant. The same principle applies here that we saw in the experiment in 1.1.3: that the important thing is to make and use one's own images.

2.2.3 BOB: Imagery and memorization

> ■ Visual, visceral and other components of meaning images.

Like Aileen, Bob was a language learner about whose overall skill or success I know nothing. Toward the end of our interview, he talked to me about memorization.

'As far as memorizing words is concerned,' Bob said, 'I don't have much trouble with that. It's best if I hear the word, and then later that evening, I'll look at it. Then I usually do the thing where I read the Turkish and block out the English, and as soon as I can block out the English and recall it once [Bob snapped his fingers], it's there. I'm very unlikely ever to forget it again.'

'You've got it then.'

'Yes,' Bob replied, 'I can read the English and visualize the Turkish, or the other way around.'

'You said "visualize." Does this mean you can see where it was on the page? That sort of thing?' I asked.

'Sometimes. But mostly it's like this. When I hear the Turkish word *okul* for "school," for example, I visualize the building, a school, the feeling of school, and that's what I try to associate with the Turkish word. The *feeling* of it, so I don't have to translate *through* English.'

'Doing it the other way would . . .'

'. . . would really mess things up. It may take me a little longer in the beginning, to associate the feeling instead of the English word, but in the long run it speeds things up. It helps my comprehension when they speak to me in class. The same thing happened to me with Spanish in Bolivia.'

'This really works for you.'

'Oh, yes, and it works for dialogs, too. I try to read the sentence in Turkish, and get the words down cold, so that I *feel* the meaning coming out of them. And then I go on and *feel* what the whole dialog is. It's like I put together a series of mental pictures.'

'And then when you say the dialog, you just talk about the pictures.'

'Exactly! And if I miss a word here or there, then I know what to focus on the next time.'

'And gradually you get it verbatim.'

'That's right.'

'And you do this primarily by forming and talking about mental pictures.'

'Yes, but I don't want to overemphasize the visual aspect. It's not so much a mental picture as a mental feeling.'

'More of a visceral than a visual thing,' I suggested.

'Yeah, almost,' Bob replied.

Comments

Bob's description of how he memorizes is clearer than Bert's. His means of memorizing is also probably somewhat different from Bert's. This excerpt illustrates two points of considerable interest to the practical learner:

- Nonverbal imagery as a whole combines many modalities: kinesthetic, visual, auditory, emotional and all the rest.[4] Out of this mass of data, some people naturally form very clear and precise visual pictures, while others are able to do this rarely or never. Bob seems to be in the second group. (So am I.) Some writers of language textbooks are excellent visualizers. Such writers often assume that everyone else is like them in this respect. When they do, they are likely to expect Bob and me to do things that we are incapable of. Bob and I, in turn, may be just a little intimidated by other people's descriptions of the vivid visual images they are seeing in their mind's eye.

■ We have just seen that some people's imagery is largely nonvisual: visceral or emotional or kinesthetic or something else. No matter what kind of imagery comes most naturally to you, it will be well worth your time to pause and associate the new foreign word or sentence directly with that imagery, rather than with some translation equivalent in your native language.

Working with the ideas

1. Suppose you needed to tell someone else how to go into the place where you live and find your shoes. On what sorts of memories would you rely most heavily? Vision? Motion?

2. How many different *kinds* of impressions do you get from a phrase like *fresh bread*, or *lumberjack*? (You should list more than just the traditional 'five senses' here!)

2.2.4 A TECHNIQUE: Meaningful memorization of text
A Bob-technique

Here are two approaches to memorizing a poem or other text in your native language:

1. Read the first line over and over until you can do it without looking at the book. Then add the second line until you can meet the same criterion, and so on until you reach the end of the poem. (Or do the same thing in writing instead of orally.)

2. Read the poem silently or aloud a time or two, *concentrating on its meaning*. Look away from the book and try to express in words the same ideas that were in the poem. Look again at the poem, comparing your wording with that of the original. Then express the ideas again in your own words, but trying to approximate the words of the original. Repeat the process until 'your wording' and the poet's wording are identical.

This second technique is more like what Bob did. Try it with a short poem in your own language. Then use what you learn from it whenever you practice sentences or texts in a language you are studying.

2.2.5 *The value of summarizing reading*

> ■ Meaning in the absence of meaning.
>
> ■ F. Rand Morton's first Spanish student.
>
> ■ BEN: Desperate need for meaning in language practice.

'Can you tell me a bit more about what happened after that first six months?' I asked.

'As we progressed through the program, and began to build up our reading vocabulary through study at home,' Bert replied, 'they began to give us textbooks that the Chinese children themselves had used. First-, second-, third- and fourth-grade readers and so on. These had all been glossed in English and explained at great length in supporting textbooks, so that we did have the necessary tools.'

'Did the things you'd been studying in the first six months consist of dialogs, or individual sentences, or some combination of these?'

'Beginning with basic dialog situations, together with a great deal of drill – systematic drills. These might just be one sentence followed by another sentence and so on.'

'So these children's books were your first contact with Chinese that hadn't been written especially for foreigners.'

'Right. Yes. Exactly. Again, the whole point being, at least as I understood it, to learn the language in the way an average Chinese would have learned it.'

'Again, your idea of the natural, childlike way to do it.'

'Yes. Here too, the ban against bringing these materials into class was maintained, so that we were expected to read them at home. We would read perhaps a lesson a day – about two pages. Then we would come to class the next day and summarize what we had read – summarize it in our own words. Then there would be give and take on the content of that. Later we used radio plays and news broadcasts in the same way.'

'Simple conversation.'

'Simple conversation with the teacher. At that point it was permitted – though not encouraged – to come in with specific problems in grammar or usage: "Why do they say this instead of that?" and so forth.'

'You asked in Chinese, or in English?'

'No, in Chinese. In fact, during the two years I was in the program, I doubt I ever heard a teacher utter a word in English. We found out only later that some of them actually knew it fairly well.'

Comments

Over the years, I have concluded that good language learning requires full and rich meanings in the learner's head. It is not enough that the learner merely know all the words in a sentence, or be able to translate it. The way Bert described the beginning of his Chinese course, I wondered about the second realm. How much meaning, really, was being paired with the sounds that he was repeating hour after hour?

There are two possible answers to this question. One is that whatever meaning he was attaching to those sentences was pale and sparse. Some students can go for amazingly long periods in this way. The most striking example I know of was the first student who completed F. Rand Morton's programmed course in Spanish, back in the 1960s.[5] This student was carefully trained in the sounds and basic grammar, plus useful phrases for asking for vocabulary and explanations. The course contained a very minimum of vocabulary, and almost no meanings. Immediately after he finished the course, the student was sent to Mexico, with a tape machine to record his interactions with the people there. Morton says that at first the Mexicans treated the student pretty much as a native-speaking moron. By the end of his stay, however, he had added so much vocabulary to his grammatical base, and become so good at handling meanings, that he was invited to lecture *in Spanish* at a university there.

At the other extreme was Ben, the very intelligent husband of a friend of my wife's. Ben came to me one day almost in tears because of exactly this spartan, meaning-free feature of a Spanish course he was taking elsewhere. Most students in that course seemed to be doing fairly well, but for him this austere and antiseptic approach was pure torture. It may be that Bert was simply at the opposite end of the spectrum from Ben.

There is a second possible explanation for Bert's success in the first months of this Chinese course. Perhaps he was just better than most people at generating his own vivid meanings for sentences that had little or no relation either to reality or to each other. He may have been like the proverbial goat living off tin cans. I have found that people vary widely in this respect.

Working with the ideas

1. What sources of meanings did Bert have in the course as he has described it so far?
2. Which features of the course would you have found most congenial? Which would you have found most difficult to get used to?

2.2.6 Paraphrasing as a learning technique

> ■ A meaning of 'communicative.'
>
> ■ 'Resolution of uncertainty' on various levels.
>
> ■ BARNEY: The power of vividly imagined conversations.

'It was very strict,' I said.

'Yes. And I repeat, it was controversial. There were others who found it not at all compatible, who in fact wanted to concentrate on translation.'

'But for you it was very suitable.'

'Very. What you got at the end was somebody who is not quite bilingual, but who has a kind of bilingual approach to things. Someone who is perhaps not as competent in written translation or in simultaneous interpreting as others might be.'

'Because in the program there was never any translation practice.'

'Right. What happened, though, was that we got to the point where we could paraphrase. The emphasis was on understanding the content, the circumstances, in Chinese, without ever translating mentally.'

'But you think that in your case, at least, the small loss in translation ability was more than offset by the fluency you gained.'

'Yes; personally, I think it worked better in the end. We could read a lot more rapidly than the people who were trained primarily in translation. We didn't stop and think about what every word means. You strive for a general grasp. Then as your vocabulary expands, you fill in the blanks. By the end of this training, I think you can both remember more content, and interpret more precisely. You're not hung up on the word-to-word correspondences.'

'By going at it in this way, you kind of built yourself a 100 per cent Chinese matrix . . .'

'Something like that.'

'. . . and anything new that came along got fitted into that matrix, rather than being pasted on by means of a translation.'

'Yes, you might put it that way.'

Comments

These days, many teachers are intensely concerned with presenting language in a 'communicative' way. In its fully developed form, this is proving to be a very productive approach to the learning and teaching of languages. We must be careful, however, not to oversimplify the meaning of 'communication.' For some, it has meant merely conveying new information, or at least resolving some genuine uncertainty in the mind of a hearer or reader. Telling the teacher 'My pen is red' is not 'communicative' in this sense if she is looking straight at the pen.[6] If she has never seen it, the same sentence is communicative (though not necessarily very interesting!). Communication in this sense certainly tends to increase the quality and the vividness of the meanings in the learner's mind.

Bert's year of Chinese at the university no doubt enabled him to translate many of the sentences in the first months of this course. The English glosses in his textbooks gave additional help. In 2.2.4 and 2.2.5, we have begun to hear about some sources for meanings that were more immediate and more vivid. One such source was the need to summarize in class what he had studied at home. Another was the opportunity to ask limited questions about grammatical points that were troubling him. A third was extensive practice in paraphrasing: in putting into his own words the contents of what he had just read or heard.

Of these three activities, only the second is clearly communicative in the strict sense I have just described. In the first, the learner is reporting to the teacher what the teacher has already read, and what she has heard dozens of other students describe in previous years. In the third, the learner is telling the teacher either what the teacher herself has just said, or what teacher and learner have just heard or read together. How can immediate or delayed paraphrasing contribute to higher-quality nonverbal mental imagery?

The answer is that a paraphrase does, after all, resolve an uncertainty. The uncertainty is not 'What is the message?' however. It is rather, 'Has the paraphraser preserved the message of the original?' In order to answer this question, both learner and teacher must compare the meanings of original and paraphrase. And in order to compare those meanings, they must have them in mind. On one level, then, I think paraphrasing is also 'communicative.' This may be why Bert was able to profit so much from it.

But even fixed dialogs or other texts *can* generate vivid meanings. All they require is more or less effort of the imagination. Concerning a Swahili sentence that he had heard in class, Barney reports:

> I spent some time making up questions I would like to ask the visitor we had last week. Then I imagined his answers. This rehearsal was done with real feeling, including imagined tone of voice and gestures. These silently rehearsed sentences, in fact, became more real to me than any I had actually heard or used in class.

Another way of getting good nonverbal imagery for fixed texts is to read them aloud while picturing a person to whom one is trying to get the meaning across. But there is no question that some people can do this more readily than others (see 5.1.1, for example). This ability may have been one requirement for success with the Audio-Lingual approach.[7]

Working with the ideas

1. In what respects is Bert 'learning' Chinese (1.1.2)? In what respects is he 'acquiring' it?
2. Which of the techniques described here have you experienced as a learner? How well did each work for you?

2.3 Notes

1. Sympathetic descriptions of the Grammar–Translation method are rare these days, but H. Douglas Brown gives a good account of it in the book I mentioned in note 3 for Chapter 1. It is also well treated in A. P. R. Howatt's *History of English Language Teaching*, published by Oxford University Press in 1984.
2. William G. Moulton's book (see Chapter 1, note 5) was in the Audio-Lingual school. Probably the most authoritative exposition of the approach was Nelson Brooks' *Language and Language Learning*, published in 1960 by Harcourt Brace. Doug Brown summarizes some more recent thinking about this approach, but it is also mentioned in all other books on language-teaching methodology. *Techniques and Principles in Language Teaching* (Oxford University Press, 1986), by Diane Larsen-Freeman, gives brief samples of Audio-Lingualism, Grammar–Translation, and a number of other methods, as well as descriptions and discussions of them.
3. The extract is taken from K. T. Schurr's and V. E. Ruble's article 'The Myers–Briggs type indicator and first-year college achievement; a look beyond aptitude test results' (*Journal of Psychological Type*, 1986 **12**, pp. 25–37).
4. Vernon Hamilton's *The Cognitive Structures and Processes of Human Motivation and Personality*, published by Wiley in 1983, is outside of the field of language learning, but it contains what I think is a very perceptive treatment of the multiplicity of modalities that enter into experience and action.
5. F. Rand Morton's exploits are described in his monograph *The Language Laboratory as a Teaching Machine*, published in 1960 by the International Journal of American Linguistics.
6. Diane Larsen-Freeman also has a chapter on the Communicative Approach, but an anthology on the subject is *The Communicative Approach to Language Teaching*, edited by C. J. Brumfit and K. Johnson and published by Oxford University Press in 1979. Brumfit later wrote an entire book about it (*Communicative Methodology in Language Teaching*, Cambridge University Press, 1984).
7. Two articles on the Myers–Briggs Type-Indicator as it relates to language learning are by Madeline Ehrman and Rebecca Oxford (*Modern Language Journal*, 1989, vol 73.1), and by Raymond Moody (*Modern Language Journal*, 1988, vol 72.4).

Chapter Three

An Informal Learner
Carla learning Portuguese and German

Carla was a young woman who had held responsible secretarial positions in a large organization in Brazil and West Germany. In each country she picked up the local language with extraordinary success, mostly outside the classroom. After her return to the United States, she took oral interview tests in Portuguese and German. Not surprisingly, the tests showed that she made certain grammatical errors, and that there were some subjects on which she could not talk at all. She was, however, able to communicate fully and comfortably on matters related to everyday life. What was even more impressive, the people who tested her reported that they felt almost as if they were talking to a member of their own culture.

Because she was planning to return to Germany, Carla was placed in a class with five people whose *overall* proficiency level was about the same as hers. Unlike her, however, the other students had learned their German during the training program. Also unlike Carla, they were officers or executives, or their wives.

3.1 Sources of encouragement

As I had expected on the basis of her high tested proficiency in both German and Portuguese, Carla had many things going for her.

3.1.1 Openness and risk-taking: two qualities of a successful informal learner

- Two qualities of a good 'acquirer.'
- The classroom as a 'frightening' place.

Carla began by talking about her general approach to language. 'It seems like I simply say what seems right – what comes out according to the circumstances,' she said.

'You don't translate, you don't mentally take two words that are related in meaning and compare them, or that kind of thing.'

'Oh, no.'

'Just the idea of *having* to *know* about the accusative case or the genitive case, or about all the various endings on the articles . . .'

Carla laughed. 'Oh, no, I have no idea about that!' she said.

'And yet you've dealt with the *language* successfully.'

'As far as I *know*,' she replied. '*I* felt I spoke much better than I evidently do speak right now. I really don't know much about understanding and memorizing rules of grammar and such. But if I just throw myself into a country, I don't know why, but I just go off and speak. I don't compare things; I don't think about language.'

'The idea of having to go at this thing on an intellectual basis – of having to learn the rules and the paradigms and so forth . . .'

'I've never done that, either in Portuguese or in German, and it's . . . it's frightening to be in this class.'

'It's frightening because of the point-by-point kind of thing, which is so different from how you actually *learned* Portuguese and German.'

'Exactly!'

Comments

Carla says she 'just throws herself into' the country where she is living. By this she apparently means that she spends her time with local people and participates in whatever activities they are engaged in. These are, of course, the conditions that small children find themselves in. We will not be surprised, then, to find that Carla's command of German is much more the 'acquired' kind than the 'learned' kind (see 1.1.2). Many theorists these days have been exploring the possibilities for acquisition by adults. They have also emphasized its great value for anyone who is approaching a new language. (In my comment at the end of this segment, I was using 'learned' in the more general, everyday sense to mean 'gained control of.')

Carla, from all reports, has been exceedingly good at 'acquiring' two different languages in this way. In order to succeed at this, an adult must have certain qualities that we have already seen in Ann. Such a person must make free and uncritical use of intuition. She or he must also have a certain kind of fearlessness about making errors. This second quality is implied by what Carla says about 'just throwing herself in.'

I was therefore surprised to hear her use a word like 'frightening' to describe her classroom experience. She confirmed my guess that what was frightening was not the language, but some aspect of the task of 'learning' in the narrow sense (see 1.1.2). We will hear more about this in the remaining segments of Carla's interview.

Working with the ideas

1. Do you find Carla's description of her approach to German and Portuguese congenial, or do you have misgivings about it? Explain your answer.
2. What might Carla find 'frightening' in her German course? Verify your guess or guesses as you read the remaining segments of the interview.

3.1.2 Looking good in the eyes of one's teachers

- Conflicts between what had been 'learned' and what had been 'acquired'.

- Differential reactions of native speakers to various aspects of learners' speech.

The supervisor of Carla's course, who was listening to the conversation, seemed surprised. 'That isn't the way it seems to the teachers,' he said. 'They all say you're doing marvellously. And you do remember,' he added, 'that I warned you the first week or two might be a little uncomfortable.'

'Yes,' Carla replied, 'but I'm groping. And all the other students know exactly which endings to put on the words, and I have no idea. If I am to pursue this course, I need to be given the ground rules: why do this and why not do that, so that when I get into class . . .'

'Even though the teachers say you're doing beautifully, still there's something almost terrifying about this . . .' I observed.

'Oh, yes!' Carla replied. 'Me, I've never memorized things. For example, the dialog we're working on now. There are certain words that the other students now know, and they can say *those* words. But I have other words or phrases that I would ordinarily use to say the same things. There are so many differences of this kind that I find it really difficult to memorize that particular dialog, and to repeat it.'

'I'm getting a picture of a bird that can naturally fly, that is suddenly brought in and is put into an experimental psychologist's machine, and told to peck here to get this, and peck there to get that,' I suggested.

'No, I don't feel that way,' Carla explained, 'because I know I speak incorrectly, and there's got to be a way of changing my way of speaking. Maybe what I need is a chance to go back and study the basic grammar, and all those charts with the *m*'s and the *n*'s and the other endings on the words.' She paused. 'Well,' she said resolutely, 'if I'm going to *go* through the rest of this course, I think I really need a basis. Because I *don't* know *why* I do the things I do.'

Comments

At the end of this segment of the interview, I said something about Carla 'learning' Portuguese and German. I was of course using the word in its everyday, general sense, rather than in the narrower technical sense of 1.1.2.

When Carla talks about 'the *m*'s and *n*'s,' she is referring to the fact that the German counterpart for English *the* consists of a list of six forms including *dem* and *den*. Speakers of German use one or another of these forms depending on the grammatical circumstances.

Carla's view of her German, and of how she was doing, was quite different from her teachers' view. They were responding to her overall good pronunciation, accent and body language, and to her use of lots of little words and phrases that hold sentences and conversations together. All this, together with her knowledge of *what* to say, and of *when*, *how* and *why* to say it, are components of a general interactive competence in the language. This is to be distinguished from mere linguistic competence: the ability to produce correct sentences. Carla's teachers must have found Carla's interactive competence in German refreshing. Carla's type of control was a typical result of 'acquisition.' She contrasted sharply with the students that the teachers were accustomed to. Their students would come to those features of German very late, if ever, because they were 'learning' – concentrating on one word or one point of grammar at a time.

Carla's impressive achievements in Portuguese and German would have been impossible without her remarkable approach to language. My suggestion about the caged bird implied that she felt good about that approach even though she was not now in a position to use it. She, however, rejected my metaphor. Clearly the approach *itself* had felt good while she was using it. But apparently she did not feel good about *having* used it.

Working with the ideas

1. I was trying to reflect back Carla's feelings toward her German instruction. Pick out the places in what Carla had said that prompted me to use the word 'terrifying.'
2. How useful have you found grammatical charts in your own study of other languages?
3. Should Carla be allowed to say things in her own words, as long as she says them correctly? Why, or why not?

3.1.3 Success with self-directed learning

> ■ Memorization of texts: deliberate vs spontaneous.
>
> ■ Challenges are not the same as requirements.

Carla had mentioned her difficulty with memorizing the dialogs in the German textbook. It turned out, however, that she did not have any difficulty with memorizing in general.

'I remember when I got out of high school,' she recalled, 'I was working at a company, and there was a Japanese man there, and I used to ask him to teach me Japanese, and he used to put Japanese on the board phonetically, and within a period of time, I had a long, legal-sized sheet of Japanese that I had memorized.'

'Memorized in the sense that you could recite it verbatim down the page?'

'Oh, no, not that.'

'But at least you could say the sentences . . .'

'Yes, things like "Would you like a cup of tea?" "The sun is shining today." Really basic things.'

'Nevertheless, you did memorize them . . .'

'He would write it in roman letters, and then we would do it, and we would learn about twenty or forty sentences.'

'So for you memorizing is fine. Even memorizing sentences that have simply been put up on the blackboard arbitrarily because you happened to think they might be nice sentences. Isolated sentences, that didn't come out of a boring conversation. That's fine as far as you are concerned.'

'No, memorizing is fun. I remember it was fun. But this . . . memorizing these dialogs is not fun. Maybe it has something to do with challenge: "Let's see how much I can learn of this person's language!" '

'You're saying that the memorizing of the Japanese sentences . . .'

'. . . was challenging and fun!'

'Whereas in German . . .'

'It's not fun. Maybe because I'm feeling pressures in the classroom situation. Or maybe because I have so many other words to express the same meaning, rather than using the particular words that are in the book.'

'Having to memorize the book's version is confining.'

'Yes. Plus, there are all those endings, and little tiny connecting words, and that bothers me too.'

Comments

My grandson at age 3½ was able to declaim verbatim the entire contents of his book about *The Three Billy Goats Gruff*. Such an accomplishment is not rare with small children acquiring their first language. But he had not set out to memorize it. I suspect that if anyone had asked him to go on and memorize *The Three Bears*, he would have refused. If he had tried, he would probably have failed. Deliberate memorization of arbitrarily selected sentences is found in 'learning,' not in 'acquisition.'

Carla is telling us of two experiences that required her to memorize sentences. One, with Japanese, had been 'fun.' The present one, with German, was 'not fun.' Three points may be significant here:

- In Japanese, Carla had helped to select the sentences. In German, they were an inflexible requirement of the course.
- In Japanese, Carla had been responding to 'challenges' that she had set for herself. In German, she was trying to meet demands that she felt were imposed by teachers and classmates.
- In Japanese, Carla had no other way to say 'The sun is shining' except the one her tutor had given her. In German, alternatives that were easily available in her head had to be suppressed. Both her teachers and she herself were implicitly denying any value to what she had already done – and enjoyed doing – in the language.

Working with the ideas

1. The commentary suggests three reasons to account for why Carla found memorizing fun in Japanese but not in German. Can you add any others? Which of these reasons do you think is most important for Carla? Which would be most important for you?
2. Have you ever found that you could repeat sentences or longer texts word-for-word (slogans, lyrics to songs, proverbs, often-repeated phrases, etc.) without ever having tried to memorize them?
   How can you draw on these experiences in learning or acquiring a new language?

3.1.4 A TECHNIQUE: Originating one's own texts
A technique from Carla

If you have access to a cooperative speaker of the language you are studying, decide on five or six things you would like to be able to say in the language. Then ask the speaker how to say them. He or she may also help you to write them down, and to pronounce them in an acceptable way.

This technique is simple but powerful. I was once working with a small French class that spent most of its time in memorizing dialogs and doing grammar drills. After we began letting students select their own sentences for a short time every day, there was a noticeable improvement in the students' fluency, and also in their attitude toward speaking the language as opposed to merely reciting it.

3.1.5 Success in socially mediated learning

- 'Thinking about' learning.
- Comparison of mental images.
- Gabelentz: 'Talkative people with a limited range of ideas.'

Carla then went back to talking about what had worked so well for her. 'Sometimes,' she said, 'I've had people say, "My, you remember that really quickly!" or "You grasped the language so well!" But I didn't feel that way. After all, I had a boyfriend there for two years, and I knew his parents, and I had other friends, and I know they used to speak to me in simple language. If my boyfriend saw there was something I didn't understand, he'd repeat it in easier language. I think other people would intentionally speak to me with simpler vocabulary, too.'

'Simpler, but still correct. So what you picked up was what they were giving you, which was genuine, but still simpler.'

'Simplified. Right! Exactly! On the other hand, there were five Germans that I toured Moscow with, and none of them spoke English, and it was really hard work for me. They thought because I could *speak* as well as I did . . .'

'They were deceived by your fluency, by the accuracy of what you did say,' I interrupted. 'They didn't know that you needed to have things restated in other ways?'

Carla agreed. 'I don't think it was the grammatical form, or the sentence structure that threw me off with them,' she said. 'It was the vocabulary. It was the words I didn't know. Because, as I said, I never paid attention to the grammatical endings anyway. When people speak to me, what they say just enters in. Even if there's a word I don't understand, of course I understand what they mean. It was the same way in Portuguese.'

'It just comes in directly, without a lot of analysis.'

'No, I don't think at all,' Carla emphasized. 'If you say something to me in German, it comes in like English. It comes in and goes out, without me ever thinking about it. In fact, I can honestly say that I don't think I've ever thought until I got into this course. Except in the beginning, when I used to sit with a dictionary.'

'But as soon as you found out you didn't have to sit with a dictionary – as soon as you got into contact with live Germans . . .'

'That's right. I didn't do any more thinking about the language.'

Comments

Carla was fortunate in finding someone who was both willing and able to rephrase things in German that was simpler, but still authentic. Some native speakers seem to have this knack naturally, while others do not. The latter quickly become discouraged and break off contact, or switch to the learner's native language if they know it. The former are a language learner's greatest asset. As Gabelentz, a nineteenth century German, put it, 'The best teachers for beginners are talkative people with a limited range of ideas'.[1] These people seem to instinctively enjoy the challenge of helping a willing foreigner to understand them.

When people saw that Carla had a surprising amount of fluency or accuracy or both, they assumed she knew more than she did. As a result, they spoke to her in language she could not follow. This is a common experience of people who are learning a foreign language. One frequent reaction under these circumstances is to feel discouraged at not being able to fulfill people's expectations. A more helpful reaction is to feel encouraged at what their expectations imply about one's progress so far. The latter seems to have been the reaction of both Ann and Carla.

We cannot be entirely sure of what Carla means by 'thinking about' language. One rudimentary kind of 'thinking about' includes the following process:

- Encounter the need to produce some grammatical feature such as a definite article (see 3.1.2).
- Notice which form 'comes naturally' (e.g., *der*).
- Recall rules or paradigms that one has already learned.
- Arrive at a form of the definite article based on that information (e.g., *dem*).
- Compare the two forms to see if they are identical.
- If the two forms are not identical, decide which to use.

For some people, this whole process takes place in a split second. For others, it requires more time and effort. For a few, like Carla, the last four steps in the sequence are either impossible or prohibitively difficult.

Working with the ideas

1. Suppose you were trying to convey the ideas in the last paragraph, above, to someone whose English was very weak. Orally or in writing, try to rephrase the paragraph so such a person would find it easier to understand.
2. *Should* Carla have paid attention to the grammatical endings while she was interacting with people? Some people *can* do this sort of thing to a certain extent. Do you think you could have?

3.1.6 CHUCK: Alternation between formal and informal exposure

- **Comprehensible input from mass media.**
- **Comprehensible input from informal contacts.**

Chuck had served as an agricultural attaché in Scandinavia, and while there, had gained quite good control of Danish. He told me about what seemed to have helped him most.

'My teacher was using some ordinary textbook,' he began. 'You know, the kind where you go through a series of dialogs. But after a certain point, I began to rely more just on television and reading the newspapers, and just going out and forcing myself to talk with people.'

'In your line of work,' I observed, 'you probably met a lot of people who didn't speak any English.'

'That's right.'

'So you just went out and put yourself into contact with the language, and . . .'

'Yep. Pretty soon it started to come. It was a combination of going through the book with the teacher, and then going out and using the stuff.'

'Just conversing with people.'

'Well, yes, but one thing that I found especially useful was just sitting down in front of the TV and just listening, being determined to understand what the guy was saying on the news.'

'That really worked for you!'

'Yeah. Of course there were times when I was ready to just pack the whole thing in and quit and go home and pack bags in the supermarket. I mean, it got *dreadful*, because Danish is a pretty ghastly language in terms of the noises they make. The Danes say they don't have a language, they have a throat disease!'

'It sounds like quite a challenge,' I said.

'Yes, sometimes I sat there watching this guy babbling, and I said to myself, "I'm never going to learn this language!" But it's remarkable. After six months, it was "All systems go"!'

'This is beginning to sound like what you told me you did with French and Italian,' I commented. 'In all three, you deliberately put yourself into a position where you were hearing not just language, but language where you understood a lot of the content. You didn't necessarily understand every word.'

'That's right.'

'But you knew enough of the language so that from what you did get of it, you were able to kind of extrapolate, and get more of it.'

'Yes, yes.'

'And this meant that you were being exposed to Danish, which consisted partly of things that you'd already mastered, and partly of things you had not mastered.'

'Yes, that's a fair summary. Sometimes you had to guess, and sometimes you guessed wrong and had to be corrected, but that was basically it. It can be a rather horrifying experience sometimes, but other times,' he chuckled, 'it can be fun!'

Comments

Like Carla, Chuck succeeded by meeting language that was hard enough for him, but not too hard. This is, of course, the way all children acquire their native language, and some theorists believe that it can be sufficient for adults also.

One must not generalize on the basis of two brief narrative accounts. Nevertheless, I can see three suggestive differences between Carla's experience with German and Chuck's with Danish:

- Danish is in some ways a more difficult language than German.
- Chuck's tested proficiency in Danish was a whole level higher than Carla's in German.
- Chuck alternated between formal instruction and informal exposure. Carla did no formal study after the very beginning of her work with German.

Working with the ideas

1. What other differences do you see between Chuck and Carla?
2. In what ways is Chuck's experience reminiscent of Ann's or Bert's?

3.2 Sources of conflict and discouragement

Almost from the beginning of our conversation, I had begun to realize that in spite of her natural ability and her past achievements, not everything was going well in Carla's present study.

3.2.1 Thoughtful vs spontaneous use of language

> ■ Etiquette and ethics of using native speakers for conversation practice.
>
> ■ Importance of the perceived attitudes of conversation partners.
>
> ■ Which *should* come first, formal or informal study?

'Another thing,' Carla went on, 'I feel *comfortable* with Germans. Sometimes I've been the only non-German in a whole group of Germans, and I don't feel intimidated. Of course,' she said, 'no one's ever laughed at me, either – or in Brazil. We'd just go ahead and do whatever we were doing. And in São Paulo we had maids, and we used to talk, talk, talk all the time!'

'At least they didn't laugh unkindly.'

'No, no! Of course everyone laughs when something's funny, but you see, nobody ever said, "Golly, you're dumb!" or made fun. And that may have helped me.'

'Even when someone did correct you, you never felt stopped in your tracks.'

'Or threatened. No. No.'

'There in Brazil, life was in Portuguese!'

'Hm! I mean, it really was!' she replied. 'I still remember quite a bit after three years. And if somebody had just sat down with me and said, "You're doing so-and-so incorrectly. Do it this way" – if they had done that repetitiously – I'd be speaking correctly today!'

Carla then began to talk about life in her present class. 'I'm really finding it difficult,' she said, 'because I'm in with people who got high scores on the aptitude test. And then there's this one fellow who knows so much *English* grammar! Most of the English grammar I know, I've picked up in studying other languages! Oh, I did have a little grammar from the Portuguese teacher I had for a while, but then I'd just come into class and close my book, and she'd start saying things to me, and I'd just close my eyes, and try not to think, and just absorb what I was learning. Come to think of it, that may be part of my problem now, having to sit down with a *book . . .*'

'It sounds as though the difficulty is that, instead of being able to close your eyes and just swap sentences back and forth, you're now being asked to deal with grammatical concepts. You're being asked to take things out of their natural German setting, and pick them up, and look at them.'

'Yes, and it doesn't feel very natural to me, to do all this.'

'Maybe the difficulty is that now you're having to introduce thinking into what, up to now, was a simple, natural process.'

Carla laughed. 'Maybe that's what it is!' she mused. 'Maybe I've started thinking!'

Comments

Which language should I use with speakers of the language I am learning? If the people I'm talking with really need to improve their command of my language more than I need to improve my command of theirs, then it would be self-indulgent for me to insist on practicing theirs with them. If my version of their language is so full of errors that they find it unpleasant to listen to or very difficult to follow, then continuing to use them as language instructors would be rude. With her maids in Brazil, Carla felt no such impediments. The maids had no pressing need to learn English, and talking with her was probably a rest from their regular chores. They were able to play the role of Gabelentz' 'talkative people with a limited range of ideas,' and Carla felt free to 'talk, talk, talk' with them.

Carla had already done a great deal of 'acquiring' of German before she began to try to 'learn' it. She has two beliefs about this. One is that it would have been better if she had done her 'learning' first: 'If only somebody had just sat down with me . . .!' The other is that she *could* have done her learning first if she had tried to. That would have meant starting out like Bert, absorbing features of German outside of their setting in German life. Was she in fact capable of doing that, I wondered? In the next segment of her interview we will find reasons to doubt it.

Working with the ideas

1. In working with other languages, how much need have you felt for conscious knowledge about the grammar of your native language?
2. Have you had any experiences in which you were uncertain which language to use with someone? How did you make your choice?

3.2.2 *Links between printed and spoken forms*

■ **Ease in reading a word does not follow automatically from ease in understanding it in speech.**

'Taking things out of context and comparing – you have trouble with things like that?' I asked.

'Really, I do!' Carla replied. 'And,' she added, 'I've never read, for example. And now for me to sit down and read is quite uncomfortable. Well, I'm beginning to feel a little more comfortable,' she said. 'But I don't visualize. For example, I know what *plötzlich* is. We use it all the time. And yet I see the word spelled in the book, and I have no connection between what I see on paper and the word I can understand when it's spoken. It was the same in Portuguese. I'd look at something and not understand it, and I'd say "Would you please read it to me?"'

'And if somebody read it aloud to you, you could understand it?'

'Perfectly!'

'But to get meaning off of the page, you almost had to read it aloud to yourself?'

Carla laughed. 'Oh, I have a very difficult time reading words, syllable for syllable, and I think to myself, "Why, *I* know that word!" But I have no visual identification of any of them.'

'Just looking at them on the page doesn't . . .'

'The word doesn't spring out at me, no. I have to dissect it. It's a feeling like I had never spoken German.'

'You mean, "Whatever language this is on the page, I've never spoken it!"?'

'Right! And I have to go through and take my time with each word, and write them down into syllables, and then finally I can say, "*I* knew that word!" Because of course I knew the word. I use it all the time. But to see it on a piece of paper, I don't recognize it at all, until I phonetically break it down.'

'A very frustrating, painful experience!'

'Oh, it's painful! It really is! It's painful to feel stupid, it's painful . . .'

'. . . to be cut off from German as you've known it?'

'Exactly!'

Comments

Carla must have been able to read and write English reasonably well. After all, she had been working as a secretary for several years. I was therefore surprised to hear how hard it was for her to interpret printed words in Portuguese and German.

One can hardly say that Carla 'read' foreign words. It was more as though she pried them off the page. This kind of herculean effort was unnecessary in chatting with Brazilian housemaids or in socializing with German friends. It would be required, however, in most language courses that concentrate heavily on academic 'learning' without much 'acquisition.' Bert could have done it without difficulty, but not Carla. Perhaps that accounted for much of her present frustration, and her feeling of being cut off from all that was comfortable in her past associations with German and Germans.

Working with the ideas

1. On what in Carla's description was I basing my word 'painful?'
2. When you remember words in your native language, do you remember them

primarily as sound, or primarily in written or printed form? Is your answer the same for words in other languages?

3. What is the most frustrating or painful part of a new language as far as you are concerned?

3.2.3 The social side of formal study: lack of confidence

> ■ Feelings about one's own performance.
>
> ■ Feelings about others' perceived feelings about one's performance.

'But as it is,' Carla went on, 'I feel restrained in the class. And on the other hand I feel *dumb*. I feel restrained because the vocabulary is there in my head, and the thought patterns are there, a little more complex than where the other students are right now. But I also feel very *dumb* because I don't know any of these endings! I don't know what I'm doing!'

'Even when you get the endings right, you don't really know them?'

'I'm guessing! I'm guessing! Or else it's a sentence that I've memorized straight from the book! I'm not . . . very comfortable in the classes.' Carla gave a little laugh.

'Pretty *un*comfortable, in fact.'

'Yeah,' Carla replied quietly. 'Part of it is all those people in there with their high aptitude scores.'

'*That's* the threatening thing,' I guessed, 'the way you think the other students must feel about you.'

'Yeah! The teachers can correct me all day long if they want to. They're fantastic, and *so* patient! But you know, if I'm in class, and stumbling over words, and all the rest of them – they *know* the stuff I'm trying to come out with, then that's a pain for them, to have to sit around because somebody else is dropping behind. I don't want to be the cause of that! And furthermore, I feel that I'm really *deteriorating* in my speaking ability because of . . . not because of the students, but because I'm . . . Well, I guess I'm tense. I'm losing my German. It doesn't fly out any more!'

Carla paused, and then went on. 'But that's not important,' she said. 'What I'm really here for is to improve my German. I wouldn't mind if I went out of here after another three hundred hours of class with the same overall proficiency score as when I came in, if I were speaking . . . correctly.'

I had an idea that Carla's grammar was not so bad as she thought. Hoping to relieve her negative feelings, I said, 'More correctly.'

'Right! "*More* correctly!" My English grammar again,' Carla responded with a sheepish laugh.

I was startled that Carla had apparently taken my words as criticism of her language. Surely she, as a native speaker of English, knew that it is perfectly correct to say 'speaking correctly.' Could it be, I asked myself, that her confidence, at least within the area of grammatical correctness, had somehow been so badly shaken that the effects spilled over even into her use of her own language? 'No, I wasn't correcting English grammar,' I said as gently as I could. 'I simply . . .' Then I found myself remembering in a new light some of the words Carla had used earlier in our conversation – words with negative emotional connotations: 'frightening,' and all the rest. I didn't finish my sentence.

Later in the conversation, Carla mentioned having studied German briefly before she went to Germany. 'In Brazil, when I learned I was going to Germany, I took about a month at Goethe. It was in São Paulo, I think one or two sessions.'

'Oh, at the Goethe Institute,' I repeated by way of confirmation.

'Oh, I'm sorry! Yeah!' she responded. Again, hearing a correction where none was intended, and even apologizing for her error.

Comments

In this segment, Carla tells us a great deal about the social side of her present language study. She feels that the other students are holding her back, keeping her from using what she knows that they don't know. At the same time, however, she feels 'dumb' because she can't use what they know and she doesn't know. She is sure her slowness produces in them at least pain, and probably resentment. She is also aware that they scored much higher than she did on the aptitude test (which was, after all, an instrument designed to test various aspects of the ability to do academic 'learning'). She is unwilling to blame the other students. Instead, she blames her own inner tension. But that tension comes largely from the way she thinks they feel about her.

Carla seems to have accepted at a very deep level the superiority of the 'learning' approach, and of its emphasis on accuracy rather than on fluency, and of people who use it: 'The fact that my ability to use German is deteriorating is not important. What is important is that I improve it.' She has also been corrected so much, or in such a way, that she hears corrections even when they are not there, and submits to them meekly.

Under these conditions, it is hardly surprising that Carla is speaking less German than before. A number of experiments have shown that even in one's native language, one tends to hesitate more and to use smaller vocabularies when one feels that one's audience is unfriendly.[2]

Working with the ideas

1. The effect of one student on another in a language class may be positive or negative. What have been your own observations on this subject?
2. Do you agree that it is better to concentrate on 'learning' before 'acquisition,' or should 'acquisition' come first? Or should they proceed hand-in-hand? Support your position by reference to your own experiences.

3.2.4 How should Carla have started her language study?

- Systematic drills are sometimes useful, sometimes inappropriate.
- Importance of recognizing and dealing with feelings in language study.
- Gradual development of language: developmental errors.
- CYNTHIA: A successful case of gradual development.

'You would give your eyeteeth to have the grammatical knowledge that these other students have,' Carla's supervisor commented, 'but *they* would give *their* eyeteeth to have the fluency and ease with German usage that you have.'

'I suppose so,' Carla replied, 'but now if I have to speak correctly, it's like undoing things that are already established.'

'Like rebreaking and resetting a leg that has been set crooked?' I wondered.

'A little bit,' she conceded.

'Actually,' her supervisor interrupted, 'the places where you make most of your mistakes are *not* places where you have formed *wrong* habits. They're places where you haven't formed any habits at all yet. It isn't that you say *die Messer* consistently when you should say *das Messer*. It's that you're about equally likely to say *der Messer*, *die Messer* or *das Messer*. So it's not so much like having to rebreak a leg. It's more like cultivating a plant that's not yet fully grown, and therefore isn't bearing a certain kind of fruit yet.'

'That's reassuring to hear,' Carla replied, 'but even being told that the teachers see this quite differently doesn't totally . . .'

'Doesn't totally relieve you of those feelings you described,' I suggested.

'No. Not at all. Not in the least,' she answered. 'Anyway, if I had it to do over, I'd come here first and study the grammar.'

'And then you'd go on to Germany and use your dependable natural ability to learn to actually *speak* the language?' I asked.

'Yes. Yes.'

Comments

What Carla's supervisor said to her here is consistent with the Natural Approach outlined in 1.1.4. According to that view, the process of acquiring a new language is a gradual one. In the early stages, one makes only the grossest distinctions with any accuracy. Later on, one becomes able to make increasingly fine distinctions until finally one talks like a mature native speaker. Cynthia's experience with English illustrates this principle beautifully:

'I was a self-taught reader of my first language [Korean] at the age of 4½,' Cynthia told me. 'But I quickly discovered that the rules I applied in order to decode written Korean did not work for many of the books I found on my dad's bookshelves.

'My initial efforts to break the secret code for non-Korean writing systems consisted of just scribbling several lines of continuous waves with dots and bars over them or across them on a piece of paper, and then to show that to my mom expecting her to read them as if they had been readable English. I couldn't understand why what I wrote wasn't readable, since they looked to me just like what I saw in those books. And when later I began to try to say things in English, I did something similar: I just uttered sounds that sounded English to my own ears. But then I came to the realization that being able to utter English-sounding sounds, or to scribble similar-looking scratches did not convey meaning to me or to anybody else.'

(My seven-year-old son learned the guitar in an analogous way, and he actually became rather good at it.)

If Carla's supervisor was right, then perhaps the solution for her problem is less difficult – less painful – than she supposed. Maybe if she had just gone on 'acquiring' German, those new differentiations and new habits would have developed in the same way the existing ones had. Or maybe all she needed was some systematic practice in the form of drills. The simplest and most traditional kind of drill for this purpose consists of repeating lists of words together with the proper form of the direct article. Other common drills require the student to choose different forms of the article according to the position of the noun in the sentence:

Cue	Expected responses	Translations
Mann	*Der* Mann ist hier.	The man is here.
	Ich sehe *den* Mann.	I see the man.
Buch	*Das* Buch ist hier.	The book is here.
	Ich sehe *das* Buch.	I see the book.
		etc.

Although drills of this kind are in disrepute among many theoreticians and practitioners today, I made good use of them when I was studying German in 1942. But Carla's discomfort with language out of context, together with her difficulty in getting printed words off the page, might have made it impossible for her to profit from them.

Carla responds to her supervisor's comments by saying, 'That's reassuring, *but . . .*' Language study is an undertaking that frequently generates strong feelings in the student. Sometimes teachers and others will understand those feelings and sometimes they will not. To be successful in this undertaking, one must be able to recognize and deal with one's own feelings without depending too much on outsiders.

Working with the ideas

1. The above commentary provides an example of a simple kind of drill. Do you think that sort of thing would be profitable in your own study of a new language? Why, or why not?
2. How closely does Carla's acquiring of Portuguese and German fit the approach

outlined at the end of the comments on 1.1.4?

3. How closely would you guess Carla fits the description at the end of the comments on 2.2.1, concerning personality type?
4. On the basis of the entire interview, what advice might you give to Carla?

3.2.5 How is Carla likely to do in the future?

> ■ 'Mistakes . . . mistakes . . . mistakes.'
>
> ■ Accounts of experiences are not always unambiguous.

Two or three times in the weeks that followed, Carla and I met by chance in the corridors. Each time, she mentioned the possibility that her current experience as a student might permanently impair her German. Two years later I received a card from her. On it, she said,

> I frankly don't think my German has improved any, mainly because I don't make the effort to read, and that for me is the only way I think I'll ever improve. At first upon returning to Germany, I was afraid of speaking, but then I fell right into it and actually I don't think I make as many mistakes as I did before I had the class. I think I unconsciously put the right endings on words. I ask people to keep an ear out for mistakes and usually when I correct myself I make a mistake the second time around, trying to correct the first time, which was correct to begin with!!! I've made many new friends here.

Comments

Do the contents of this postscript provide a happy ending to Carla's story, or an unhappy one? Readers have disagreed on this question. I am not sure which conclusion to draw.

Working with the ideas

1. How does Carla exemplify or contradict the criteria listed by Carroll (see 1.1.1) and by Omaggio (see 1.2.6)? Cite evidence from her interview.
2. Do you think Carla's story ends happily, or unhappily? Support your conclusion with quotations from the interview.
3. What questions would you still like to ask Carla?

3.3 Notes

1. This quotation from Gabelentz is taken from Otto Jespersen's classic *How to Teach a Foreign Language* (London: George Allen and Unwin, p. 74), the English translation of which was first published in 1904, but it is still reprinted from time to time.
2. This research is summarized on p. 63 of my *Memory, Meaning and Method*, which Newbury House first published in 1976.

Chapter Four

An Imaginative Learner
Derek learning German, Russian and Finnish

Derek was a middle-aged executive who had already been highly successful with German and Russian. He was also doing very well in his current study of Finnish, but as we will see, Finnish turned out to be a very different experience from German or Russian. Derek's approach to the task also proved to be quite unlike the approaches of Ann, Bert or Carla. Throughout the interview Derek spoke deliberately, appearing to think carefully about each answer as he gave it.

4.1 Imagination in mastering fundamentals

To me, the most striking thing about Derek's approach to languages was his high degree of originality and imagination. This showed up first in his learning of grammar.

4.1.1 Devising one's own tables of forms

- **What works with one language may not work with another.**
- **Importance of learner accepting responsibility for own progress.**
- **'Stockpiling' grammatical forms.**

'I arrived expecting Finnish to be difficult,' he began, 'and I'd say at the end of 4½ months that the claims were not exaggerated. It's quite difficult in comparison to German, or even to Russian.'

'Those were the languages you had studied previously?'

'Yes. And I soon realized I'd have to find some way of handling certain aspects of

Finnish grammar. I don't recall such a thought in regard to either German or Russian. I was able to just take those languages as they were presented.'

'You discovered that this time, you'd have to find a way for yourself.'

'Yes. For example, I can cite one technique that I don't recall having used in either German or Russian. It was to devise tables which would present to me all of the significant inflections of the nouns and the verbs.'

'Devise tables?' I thought. 'Carla could never have done this! And there's no evidence that Ann or Bert did, either.' 'Inflections,' I repeated. 'You mean the basic form of a noun or verb with all its endings and combinations of endings.'

'That's right. And these tables let me see on one sheet of paper what was happening in the structure.'

'You got a bird's-eye view,' I said.

'Yes. And by so doing I was able to isolate what, for my memory process at least, were key distinctive features.'

'That is, the features that you had to notice if you were going to keep track of what was going on.'

'Exactly. I found that taking say, the declensions of the noun, I had to deal with them one at a time. There are so many of them in Finnish – there are so many types of endings depending on what sort of stem you have. And an additional complication of Finnish is that the whole word can be transformed depending on the ending. The visual shapes of the inflected forms may bear very little resemblance to the nominative form that you find in the dictionary.'

'That *does* sound complicated,' I agreed.

'Yes. So at that point, quite early on, I got into drawing up these tables for myself, which then helped me to isolate the pattern, and to categorize the nouns by families. And consequently when I came to the practical use of the word, I was able to recall that it belonged to that family, and once having made that identification, it helped me to get a grip on the whole set of forms.'

Comments

Ann, Bert and Carla described their own learning styles, and the methods that had worked for them. In this opening segment of his interview, Derek says something that represents a quiet breakthrough. Everyone knows that languages are different from one another, and that some are harder than others. Derek is telling us here that they also differ with regard to the *ways* in which they are hard. It would not have worked, he says, simply to have applied more vigorously the same techniques of learning that had worked so well in German and Russian.

So Derek did not say, 'I did well in two other languages. Therefore my slower progress in Finnish must be due to shortcomings of the teachers or the textbook.' Instead, he decided that, '*I'll* have to find a way of handling the situation – a way that is suitable for *my* memory process.' He accepts primary responsibility. Like Bert, he recognizes that what works for his 'memory process' may not be suitable for other learners.

In this segment, Derek is talking about stockpiling not words, but grammatical forms. Moreover, this way of dealing with Finnish grammar seems to be fundamental to his study, and *not just an added optional help*. For Derek, his construction of the tables is one means of building up his mental resources for a very important linguistic task – the task of coming up with the right endings at the right times.

Working with the ideas

1. Where are the worst complications in the language you are studying now, or in one you have studied?
2. How do you think Ann, Bert and Carla would have reacted to the idea of making charts? How would you feel about undertaking such a project?

4.1.2 A contribution of 'learning' to 'acquisition'

> ■ **Active search for abstractions.**
>
> ■ **Apparent contribution of 'learning' to 'acquisition'.**
>
> ■ **Feeling of things 'slipping into place'.**
>
> ■ **DONNA: Benefit from organizing and memorizing.**

'You've apparently had very practical results from the intellectual activity of putting the tables together,' I observed.

'Oh, yes! For instance, in one of the cases of Finnish, it helped me that I noted mentally that if you had a double vowel in the ending of the singular, you had a different double vowel in the plural.'

'An abstract observation, but you found it useful.'

'Yes. Or with the verbs it became absolutely essential for me to know that the key to the whole thing was the simple past tense. If I memorized that and the infinitive, I would not have any difficulty, usually, with any other part of the verb.'

'Simple, but you would have been lost without it.'

'That's right. What I'm trying to illustrate is that there was a certain mental search process – a search for mental crutches. But I think it went beyond that. The crutches weren't just arbitrary. They do have something to do with the way the language behaves.'

'You made them up, but you had to check them against reality.'

'Yes, and it turns out that Finnish seems to have underlying it a type of mathematical structure, so that by writing the words out, and lining them up in the correct way, I got visual patterns.'

'This must have taken a certain amount of experimentation, followed by a bit of insight.'

'True. But what I found was that I had to line them up in a vertical column, with the last letter of each form under the last letter of the form above it.'

'What in typing is called "right justification"?'

'Yes, that's it. And it seemed to me that once I had done this, it was like inputting into my own mind. It wasn't something that I visually recalled when I was trying to decline a word. It was a way of *putting the information in* – into my mind. I had a feeling – almost a physical feeling – that "OK, that was enough, the information had gone in and it was there." '

'A physical feeling of . . .'

'Of having absorbed it. Yes.'

'Sort of slipping into place?'

'Something like that, yes.'

Comments

Derek's 'active search process' fits the second of Omaggio's characteristics of successful language learners (see 1.2.6). This search leads him to notice and keep track of some rather abstract linguistic matters. For example, he talks about 'declensions' and 'conjugations,' and the doubling of vowel sounds. Some learners would find this a bit formidable. It is certainly 'learning' rather than 'acquisition' (see 1.1.2)!

Donna's story is similar to Derek's. She had had a relatively successful experience with French, which she studied in school for three years beginning at age twelve. When she was twenty-four, she found that her French was still serviceable during a week-long vacation in a French-speaking area. The method used in her classes involved the memorization of dialogs, but it also included a great deal of explicit grammar study. The pupils were required to keep notebooks that were both extensive and neat. Donna felt that the experience had made her into a better-organized person overall. It left her, she said, 'with a sort of filing system in my brain. As a result, the mention . . . of the infinitive form of a verb would instantly awaken in my mind every form of that verb in its present-tense conjugation with various subjects, and in its past and future tense conjugations as well. In fact, I recall *making little study sheets* prior to a test so as to have everything neatly organized. By the time I had written these drills all out, *I no longer needed to study*. My memory was fixed, and it was just a matter of regurgitating it back onto paper the next day.'

'But didn't the information evaporate within forty-eight hours after the test?' I asked Donna. 'No,' she replied, 'I had it available *as long as I continued to use the language*.' From what Donna said about herself, she sounds like a relatively successful 'stockpiler' (see 1.2.5)!

Ann found the stockpiling of words to be distasteful and prohibitively difficult. Bert, in his work on Chinese, was stockpiling mostly sentences. Now Derek and Donna are talking about stockpiling not words and not sentences, but grammatical forms. For them, their construction of the charts is one means of building up their mental resources for a very important linguistic task – the task of coming up with the right endings at the right times.

Working with the ideas

1. In this segment of his interview, Derek begins to tell us about his work with charts. Which part of the process do you think would be most difficult for Carla? Why?
2. Whether in learning language or in learning some other skill, have you ever had Derek's experience of feeling that a new component of the skill had *at a certain moment* almost physically 'slipped into place'?

4.1.3 A TECHNIQUE: Learning grammar with cuisenaire rods
A technique from Derek and Donna

Here is a technique that takes advantage of the value of visualizing grammatical forms and of manipulating them physically. I have found it to be particularly effective with students who have a little trouble dealing with grammatical abstractions in the usual academic ways. The technique works best if you have access to a set of cuisenaire rods (sometimes called math rods or Algebricks), which are available in many educational supply stores.

■ Take one of the longer rods (a blue one or an orange one) and set it on the table in front of you. This rod will stand for the stem of the noun or verb whose forms you are trying to learn.

■ If the grammatical forms you are studying involve suffixes, place a different color of rod to the right of that rod, to stand for each grammatical category you are working with. For example, if you are trying to learn genitive, dative, accusative and ablative cases for nouns or adjectives, one 1 cm (white) rod might stand for genitive singular, and two 1 cm rods would stand for genitive plural. Similarly one 2 cm (red) rod could stand for dative singular, and so on. When you have all the rods set up, they will look something like those in the diagrams:

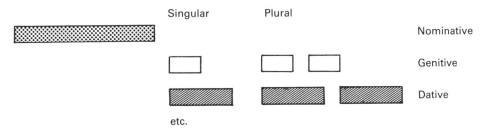

■ Point to a combination of rods, and try to give the correct form. Pointing to the single white rod means 'genitive singular,' pointing to the two 2 cm rods means 'dative plural,' and so forth. Pointing to the long rod on the left means 'choose a new noun.' Check yourself, or better yet, have a partner check you.

This technique commonly starts out fairly slow and careful, but then becomes quite lively after a few minutes.

4.1.4 Sometimes working from chaos to order

- ■ Awareness of specific gaps in one's own understanding.

- ■ How to ask and answer questions about grammar.

Derek's doughty forays into the thickets of Finnish grammar fascinated me. 'And were most of these observations, these generalizations, already in the textbook,' I asked, 'or were they mainly things that you worked out for yourself?'

'Well, it was a combination of both. I would say that the instructional approach in this course is very much concerned with not frightening the student, and consequently it seems to me there is a reluctance to bring grammatical questions to the forefront.'

'For fear of overwhelming the student?'

'Yes. But later on in a dictionary I discovered that the Finns themselves group them into fifty-three families.'

'You mean the Finns have been doing this all along, but you discovered it for yourself!'

'Well, of course my own groupings were a little different. I grouped them the way *I* wanted to. The Finnish dictionary was much more comprehensive, and it took note of changes that were so obscure that they would be uninteresting for the ordinary individual.'

'So if they *had* been presented to you, they might not have been quite as helpful as the ones that you worked out for yourself?'

'Yes, I think that's right. If someone had thrown it at me – and they could have – it's in one of the books – if someone had started with that, I think it would have turned me off, because you're asked to look at things that are very detailed and very subtle, and it would be an awkward way to start. To immerse you in it and let you find your way out – that's the way to go.'

'Pretty much what happened in your case,' I observed, 'in that you were immersed in it, and people almost withheld the type of information which you later found so useful for yourself. But if they hadn't withheld it – if they had given it to you in their own form and in their own time – it might have been just as undesirable as they seemed to fear it might be.'

'Yes. I think their intuition on this matter has been correct. But on the other hand, it does raise a problem for a person who is so immersed that he doesn't find his way out.'

'A person who doesn't find it the way you did.'

'Of course in my case, whenever I get to the point where I need an explanation, or want to be sure one of my formulations is not going to create more exceptions than it accounts for, the teachers have been very able and willing to go over it and explain it or correct it.'

'You did need the teachers at those times.'

Comments

Derek makes up his own charts and generalizations. He says he gets more value from doing so than from having the same material presented to him by a teacher or a textbook. This is the same principle we found at work with Ann (1.1.3). A teacher would be able to find many gaps in the resources that Derek has available for producing Finnish nouns and verbs. But only Derek knows which of these gaps he feels ready to work on right now.

In my own learning, I have observed something that I suspect is related to this principle. Sometimes I ask questions of a teacher, or of someone else, about how a language works. When I do so, I usually find that most of the value in the answer comes in the first five seconds. In asking my question, I am trying to find a missing piece in a jigsaw puzzle that I was putting together in my head. If the 'answer' goes on much longer, it often begins to get into matters that are no longer adjacent to that missing piece, so it is no longer an answer. When that happens, I begin to get lost. The antidote seems to be to keep control of the conversation by asking very specific questions *of my own*. Many of my students have seemed to react in the same way to my long explanations.

Working with the ideas

1. How would you go about explaining the irregular verbs of English (*sing–sang–sung*, *see–saw–seen*, etc.) to someone who asked you about them?
2. Derek recommends that students be immersed in a problem, and then allowed to try to find their own way out of it. How would you react to being treated in this way?

4.1.5 Mental files and indexes

> - **Learners differ in what works and doesn't work for them.**
> - **The Cognitive Audio-Oral Bilingual Approach.**

'Oh, yes, of course,' Derek replied. 'And I used the same technique – chart-making – not just with the noun declensions and the verb conjugations, but also with some of the horribly complicated parts of Finnish vocabulary. And I found no published materials that even touched these problems in the vocabulary.'

'You were exploring new territory, then.'

'As far as I knew, I was. But I think that both student and teacher have to be willing to face these things.'

'To face them and deal with them,' I said.

'Absolutely. I think it would be good to set aside a day or two for each of these topics, and just announce that "today we're going to concentrate on thus-and-so." This is unlike the approach that is taken in our present course, which is to learn these things by using them. The idea seems to be that you will pick them up by repetition, by using certain phrases, without being terribly conscious of all the changes. But I prefer to see the changes. I think once I *see* them I'm better able to retain them.'

'You're much more comfortable when you can see such things in the open, and work with them consciously.'

'Oh, yes. Now, I'm not trying to say that I'm against the conversational approach to language learning, or that I want to turn us all back to just grammar.'

'You do feel that the conversational approach has its place.'

'Oh, sure! I think it must continue to be the main vehicle – 90 per cent of the course – because it obviously works. But at least in Finnish, because of the exceptional intricacies of the grammar . . .'

'You feel a little more aggressiveness is needed on the part of the teacher?'

'Yes. Neither student nor teacher should be afraid to face the difficulties. Some people seem to think we should learn a foreign language as adults the same way we learned our native language when we were children. But we have to learn languages more in the way we learn other things as adults, and there is more method and more system. We do have mental files and we do have indexes. Why deprive a person of these skills? Let them use them in learning language!'

Comments

At the beginning of the interview, Derek recognized that his 'memory process' might be different from some other people's. Now, however, he is saying that 'we' have mental files and indexes. In effect, he is assuming that everyone is like him in this respect. Successful people often slip into this way of talking, whether about language study, or about learning some other kind of skill. When the successful language learner is also a teacher who is writing a textbook or planning a lesson, such an assumption often leads to disappointment.

And if the successful learner is a student, he or she may become impatient with other students who seem not to be making proper use of those supposedly universal mental faculties! Some of this may have been going on in Carla's German class. At least she seemed to fear it was.

In 1.1.4, I listed the steps that an adult language student should go through according to the 'Natural Approach.' What Derek has just said is in many ways inconsistent with that list. In fact, Derek's preferences are much more closely in line with another approach, called the 'Cognitive Audio-Oral Bilingual (CA-OB) method.'[1] According to this approach, the five steps in classroom learning of a new language are as follows:

■ *Identification* of the new item: what it is, how it sounds and looks, etc.
■ *Reproduction* of the new item, either silently or aloud.
■ *Understanding* of what the new item does, and how it relates to other items in the language.
■ *Manipulation* of the new item, first (and often briefly) in a mechanical way, and then in connection with appropriate meanings.
■ *Application* of the new knowledge (putting the new item to real or realistic use).

Working with the ideas

1. Pick out the places in this segment where Derek seems to be working by the CA-OB method rather than by the Natural Approach.
2. Some learners need very little help in developing their own understanding of how a new language works. Others need much more. For you, does the difference between these two groups carry any connotation of moral qualities such as 'strength of character,' or 'self-reliance'?

4.1.6 Forming and testing hypotheses

■ **Active search leads to better retention.**

■ **The process may be more important than the written product.**

■ **The learner as author and protagonist.**

I wondered what I would have done with such charts. 'And once you had made the charts, did you sit down and contemplate them?' I asked. 'Did you read them aloud to yourself . . . ?'

'It was more like contemplating them. I never tried to memorize a chart as such.'

'Or even read it aloud very much?'

'No. The learning was 90 per cent accomplished, I think, just in the doing. If I could get it into chart form, it meant to me that I had learned it.'

'The making of the chart even more than the contemplating of the chart?'

'Yes.'

'You would probably make a draft of the chart, and look at that and see if you couldn't improve it, but it was exactly this sort of cognitive labor that caused things to, as you put it, kind of click into place, and almost physically become a part of you.'

'Mhm. That is exactly the feeling I would have on those occasions, because it would be like establishing a hypothesis, and then I would try it out in various situations, and when it didn't fit, I'd learn something. So I became conscious of what was going on.'

'That was where the learning was. It was in the guessing, testing, revising, guessing, testing, revising.'

'Mhm. As a matter of fact, I would seldom refer to the charts after I had finished making them.'

'You had no need to.'

'That's right. It soon becomes more like a mental possession. But I should emphasize that it all depended on having compatible, encouraging, interested teachers.'

Comments

Derek's 'active mental search' (4.1.2) leads him to form hypotheses – guesses – about how the language works. He then tests his hypotheses by seeing whether they hold up when he meets new words and phrases in Finnish. When they do not work, he happily changes them or discards them altogether. In these respects he fits Carroll's and Omaggio's descriptions of successful language learners (see 1.1.1 and 1.2.6). If Derek's study of Finnish were a drama, he would see himself as both the protagonist and the author, with the teachers as directors and supporting players.

When he had perfected a chart as much as he was able, Derek did not study it. He simply put it aside. In this respect he is again like Donna (4.1.2).

Working with the ideas

1. Not everyone is like Derek and Donna, who are willing to discard the charts they have put together with so much effort. Would that kind of behavior be right for you?
2. Go back and look at your explanation of English irregular verbs (4.1.4). Try to improve it.

4.1.7 Vigorous mechanical drill

- ■ **The metaphor of 'cards in one's deck.'**
- ■ **Rassias and 'Dynamic Intimidation.'**
- ■ **DONNA: Organization and memorization again.**

What Derek had said about charts made me wonder how he felt about some of the more mechanical styles of language study. 'What about drill-type materials?' I asked.

'Both in Finnish and in other languages, have you found these to be very helpful, or not very helpful, or . . .?'

His answer surprised me. 'I'd rank them at the very top of anything that has helped me to learn languages,' was Derek's immediate reply. 'In particular, I rank teachers in terms of how exhausted and limp they leave me. I see a correlation in my own learning process. I learn more on the days when I'm really tired and beat down. Personally, I am left much more limp by these drills than by anything else.'

'Limp, but very much helped?'

'Helped in the way major surgery helps. It's unpleasant . . .'

'Like vigorous calisthenics, but a few days later, you're stronger,' I suggested.

Derek seemed to accept my comparison. 'I know it's good for you,' he went on. 'I actually feel myself learning. At the beginning, I was conscious of myself searching out the right ending from among all the possibilities.'

'A lot of mental activity!'

'But then toward the end of the drill period, you're too tired to think, and if you get it right, you get it right only because you had learned it. The path has been formed, and once formed correctly, it will never be forgotten.'

'It has put another card into your Finnish deck.'

'Yes. It's there and will always be there, and you'll reach for it, and you're going to come up with it, or at least most of the time. But the worst thing for me is if it's confused when it goes in – if I misunderstand an explanation, for example. Once I put anything in, it's hard to get it out. But if you get it right the first time, you don't need a lot of review.'

Comments

Physically exhausting drill was a key element in the Audio-Lingual Method, which was most widely used between about 1955 and 1965 (see 2.1.1) but is still widely practiced today. Audio-Lingual drill was based on the belief that repetition 'forms paths.' For example, if what was repeated was a sentence, then that same sentence would be easier to say after the repetition than it had been before the repetition. Or a drill might require students to change a series of affirmative sentences into negative sentences. It was expected that after such a drill, the student would find it easier to produce negative sentences than before it.

John Rassias is a highly regarded program director, who has on occasion jokingly referred to his method as 'Dynamic Intimidation', Rassias used to warn his teachers that if they and their students were not exhausted at the end of a drill session, he would not consider that they had done a good job.[2] Many students disliked that sort of activity, though many others seemed to thrive on it. Derek, like Bert, not only can tolerate it, but actually seems to profit greatly from it. And Donna, whom we met in 4.1.2, provided a series of recommendations for teachers, based on her own experience as a learner. The last three items in her list were:

- Have students record in writing, in an organized fashion, all structures being used.

- Emphasize contrastive analysis.
- Drill, drill, drill!

Working with the ideas

1. Do you think Derek would agree with the slogan 'No pain, no gain'? What evidence can you find in this segment of his interview?
2. Derek and Donna seem quite emphatic about the value that they found in mechanical drills. How easy is this for you to believe? What in your past experiences influences your answer?

4.2 Imagination in using the language

Derek also showed great imagination in how he managed to put the language into use, and in the ways in which he ensured that he attached meanings to forms.

4.2.1 'Starter words'

> - **Ways of maintaining momentum when conversation with native speakers lags.**
>
> - **DENISE: Social reasons for trying to minimize foreign accent.**
>
> - **DAOUDI: The importance of getting rhythm as well as vowels and consonants.**

Derek switched to a new topic. 'It seems to me there are such things as what you might call "starter words,"' he said. 'I've noticed these in all languages. They seem to trigger words and phrases that unleash thought. I find that once I get a few of them, it's a lot easier to talk. For example in Finnish, one that I've picked up is the phrase that means "That is to say." What it does for me is that it lets me be brief and simple, and get out quickly what I want to say. It may not even be comprehensible, but I get enough of it across to the other person, that he's at least got something to hold on to. Then I signal with this phrase that more's coming, don't interrupt, don't ask me questions yet.'

'It's a way of holding the floor. It buys you some time.'

'More than that. These phrases seem to help give form to my thoughts. Part of the process lies in being something like an actor. If I can get someone else's lines, lines that seem to work for a native speaker in a native situation, and if I can see how he is using his lines, I'll find a way to use them repeatedly in my own conversation. Of course, they'll be a little hackneyed . . .'

'You mean that in a conversation, you not only pick out sounds and say, "Ah, that's the way to pronounce it," but you also notice words and phrases that might come in handy later on and then, a minute or an hour or a day later, you have access to this. And this is easier to do when you use those little "starter phrases" like the one you just mentioned.'

'Yes, I find myself needing them, asking for them, asking "Where are they?" in a language. They help in the transition from my thoughts to words that others can understand.'

'It's almost like in a railroad train. If you didn't couple the cars together and just pushed them down the track, they might bang into each other or drift apart, whereas with these little phrases it makes your conversation into real language-use, rather than being just a verbal performance.'

'Exactly! And it seems to have this effect on my interlocutors also. As you go from one language to another, the sheer exhaustion that follows the first time you use the language in a social evening is hard to describe! And it works in the other direction also. I think we leave the native speakers as worn out as we are.'

'If in fact they don't walk off and leave us first!' I added. We both laughed.

'So I have decided the more help we can give the native speakers by adapting our speech patterns to theirs, the more at home they feel,' Derek concluded.

'We learn from them, but if we want them to stay with us, we ought to do what we can to help them to endure us!'

'Yes!'

Comments

Other 'starter phrases' in English might be 'as you said a moment ago,' or 'at least from one point of view,' or 'be that as it may.' They help to give shape to the conversation without contributing to its actual content. From what Derek said, 'buying time' is only one of their uses. I suspect that they also help to bring back associations with previous occasions when the language has been used. In any case, I've talked with other people who use such phrases in very much the same as Derek did, though they call them something other than 'starters.'

Trying to speak a new language can bring discouragement and fatigue. Learners and teachers alike are aware that this is true for the person who is trying to speak. Derek reminds us that native speakers can suffer from it too. Here is how this sort of exchange looks to Denise, a native speaker of French:

When I am learning a new language, I try to have just as little foreign accent as possible. There are two reasons for this. One comes from my contacts with foreigners who were speaking French. I sometimes found their pronunciation very comical. I wouldn't actually laugh out loud at them, but I felt as though I was doing them a favor by taking the time to let them struggle with the language. I would usually become quite impatient and 'tune them out,' or I'd try to finish the sentence so that we could get on with the conversation.

The other reason why I'm so concerned with pronunciation was that in dealing with foreigners, I found that their knowledge of grammar and vocabulary didn't make a big difference. The heavier their accent, the less they were understood. So I have concluded that for me, learning pronunciation is just as important as learning grammar, if not more so.

Daoudi, a South Asian, seems to have used this principle to good advantage:

I learned Farsi in Iran. In my early attempts to get the pronunciation, I was making (or at least thought I was making) the same sounds as they were, but I was totally incomprehensible to them. Then I decided to use my ears to pick up the rhythm of their language. Once I started speaking Farsi in their rhythm, I was comprehensible to them even though sometimes my vowels and consonants were a little different from theirs.

I also found that, though my Farsi vocabulary was not very extensive, my speech appeared to be more acceptable to them than the speech of several other people from my part of the world. This was true even though those other people had better vocabularies than I did. I don't think I would have tried as hard as I did to improve my Farsi if I hadn't had frequent need to communicate with Iranians.

While I was writing this book, I showed the interviews with Ann, Bert and the rest to a number of language teachers. I had expected that they would find Derek's rather earnest, systematic approach to language learning dull in comparison with the others. I was therefore surprised to find that many of them very strongly identified with Derek with regard to their own experiences *as learners*. In any case, as we shall see in the next segment of this interview, he was not just a mechanic. He also had quite a fertile imagination.

Working with the ideas

1. In your experience, how do most speakers of your native language react to strong 'accents' in the speech of foreigners? Why do you think they react in this way?
2. What are some 'starter phrases' in a language you have studied, or are studying?

4.2.2 An imaginary brother

- 'Liveliness,' 'meaning' and 'communication.'
- Difference between 'talking about' and 'assuming the role of.'

'Here's another technique you might be interested in,' Derek said. 'In class, on a daily basis, it's often hard simply to think of things to say. In the beginning, it's something like stage fright, and then you're just plain bored. There's a tedium to the conversation-practice sessions which afflicts the teachers as well as the students.'

From my experiences both as a learner of languages and as a teacher, I thought I recognized exactly what he was talking about. ' "Now it's time for conversation. What shall we say?" '

'Mhm! It goes against our natural grain to talk when we don't have anything to say. But what I found myself doing was that I created a fictitious brother, and made his character rather colorful and flamboyant. He would get into difficulties, and say crazy things, which relieved me of the onus of responsibility for anything I said or thought.'

'You spoke as if you were your brother?'

'No, I would begin my conversation time by telling something *about* my brother. Then we might go on and talk about something else, but it gave us a start.'

'It gave you a release from the tedium and unnaturalness.'

'Yes, and it let me find ways to use words better. Suppose I had just been taught a set of words and phrases about riding a bus. If I hadn't been on a bus recently, it was hard for me to use them in speaking for myself. But by transferring all this to an admittedly fictitious situation, I could use whatever words or phrases had been taught to me.'

'Kind of a surrogate reality – a surrogate identity.'

'Exactly!'

'It's fictional, but it still has enough continuity so that your imagination can be freed from being tied to the ground.'

'Yes. I notice great differences in my speaking ability depending on whether I'm interested in what I'm trying to say.'

'Or whether it's just time to make some more sentences.'

'Exactly! When it's the latter, everything just goes downhill.'

Comments

A question may serve to make a conversation livelier if the person who is questioned has something interesting to say on the topic, or the person questioned thinks the questioner is really interested in the answer, or (preferably) both. Some people need both these conditions if they are to converse freely. Others find it easy to talk if what they are saying interests them, even when the questioner is obviously not interested in the answer. But a question that meets neither of these two conditions slows a conversation down. One such question is the language teacher's old standby Monday gambit, 'What did you do over the weekend?' This question seldom meets both the conditions I have just mentioned. Derek's 'brother' released him from actual fact, which is often dull. This device also allowed Derek to express sides of himself that his age and professional status would have required him to suppress. In both these ways, the 'brother' opened up new possibilities in regard to the first condition.

But if a conversation is about a fictitious brother, is it really communicative (see 2.2.6)? I think it can be. 'Communication' means the accurate transfer of an image from one mind to another. The source of the original image – whether history or fiction – is relatively unimportant. What is more important is to check and verify that what has been received is consistent with what was sent.

Working with the ideas

1. Derek might also have assumed the role *of* another person, instead of just talking *about* him. Which do you think would be easier for you? Why?
2. What conditions make it easier or more difficult for you to engage in small talk in your native language? Can you think of any specific occasions that illustrate your answer?
3. In your opinion, did Derek's talk about his 'brother' contribute more toward his 'interactive competence,' or toward his 'linguistic competence' (see 3.1.2)?

4.2.3 Relating available forms and available meanings

> ■ **'Fossilization.'**
>
> ■ **Derek's maxim: 'If you can't learn to say what you want to say, learn to want to say what you can say.'**

Then Derek surprised me. 'I think I'm against originality in speaking a foreign language,' he said.

'*Against* originality?!'

'Yeah, as far as the real world is concerned. What is important for me, particularly in the early phases, is to know that I have said something right once. That constitutes a card in my deck for Finnish or whatever language. And if I know enough about the grammar to manipulate the endings, I will try to use that again. I will even go so far as to say, "If you cannot learn to say what you want to say, then learn to want to say what you can say." By that I mean, do not feel that your objective is to be able to translate your pure thought into pure Finnish. Be willing to be a little pedestrian. Get a certain stock of things even if they sound a little trite to you.'

'This is where your brother came in handy. He allowed you to want to say things that you could say.'

'Yes. Yes, I had a context where I could play around with things that I knew well. It set limits for the possible, but it still allowed room for spontaneity, which is important, at least to me. It gives me something to talk about that you don't already know. And as adults, we don't ordinarily talk without that. It wears everyone out.'

'As you say, both the teacher and the student need to have some sort of support and some source of energy, and artificial conversation can drain off energy pretty fast.'

'Absolutely!' Derek agreed. 'I don't think there is anything harder than the work of learning languages. It's never been easy for me!'

'You've been successful, but with considerable hard work.'

'It has never been an unconscious learning process. It has always required a structured approach,' Derek replied.

'Going back to your "brother",' I said, 'Do you think it would have been just as good to work with a printed dialog that was on the same subject as what you had talked about in one of your conversations about your brother?'

'No, I don't think so. It has something to do with intensity or spontaneity. You know, if you read a magazine or a book, you'll never be able to say it in the same way, because it was not imprinted on you that way. There's a difference between passivity and activity, between receiving something and making it. I think the connections are left in our minds only when *we* make the sentence.'

'That is to say, you were limited by the Finnish cards in your deck, and if you had to stick to objective reality you were limited by the things that you had to say, and these two sets of limitations interacted on one another, and sometimes between them, they just about choked off all the possibilities.'

'That's a good way to describe it, because until I hit on the "brother" idea, I frequently found myself reaching for cards that weren't there.'

Comments

In the Natural Approach (see 1.1.4), students are exposed to lots of talk that they can understand. Then, when they are ready, they begin to say things on their own, in order to communicate with other people. At no time do they focus on one grammatical point – on one set of choices – or on language as language. In this way, they gradually improve their proficiency in the language. Carla was a clear example of this process.

But how long and how far will the language of people who study in this way continue to improve? Carla's supervisor (3.2.4) seemed to think that with continued exposure she would eventually come to control all of those 'little endings' that were giving her so much trouble at the time. All too frequently, however, we meet people who have not yet picked up some of the most fundamental features of a language that they have been hearing around them for years or even decades. Instead, certain errors seem to have become permanently and inflexibly embedded in their speech, something like fossils in a rock formation.

One way of preventing this kind of 'fossilization' is through the use of drills. This was typical of Audio-Lingualism (1.1.4). Other methods, including the classic Grammar–Translation method, relied on intellectual understanding. The CA-OB method (4.1.5) employs both of these devices.

In this segment of his interview, Derek shows his affinity for the CA-OB method, according to which language students should be encouraged to be conceptually creative only with elements they know thoroughly, following rules that they know thoroughly. In a course taught by this method, the learner at all times knows what is going on, and knows the basis for the limited choices facing him or her. The likelihood of fossilized incorrect forms is reduced.

So Derek says, '*If you cannot learn to say what you want to say, then learn to want to say what you can say.*' He is here recommending the disciplined and conscious use of two resources: not only the vocabulary and grammar that one has available; but also the motivations and purposes that one might adopt. This strikes me as an outstanding maxim, both for wisdom and for practicality.

This segment of the interview contributed toward my idea of Derek as a person. I was interested to hear that so successful a learner still found languages such hard work. I also had a hunch that if he were playing bridge or poker, he would be an expert card-counter.

Like Ann (1.1.3), Derek illustrates the value of working from one's own mental imagery rather than from imagery provided by someone else.

Even more clearly than in 4.2.2, Derek here emphasizes the effect that various activities can have on the energy level of native and non-native speakers alike.

Working with the ideas

1. Here are some purposes that people sometimes have. Which are more common when a person is being a language student than when one is not?

to amuse	to amaze
to speak correctly	to sound friendly
to deceive	to get a job done
to persuade	to give accurate information
to arouse curiosity	to evaluate

   How could you introduce some of the other purposes into your work as a language learner?
2. Derek uses the metaphor of 'cards' in his 'deck' of resources for speaking and understanding Finnish. Does this metaphor appeal to you intuitively? Why, or why not?

4.2.4 DEXTER: Making vocabulary stick

> ■ Visual, but non-eidetic, memory for printed words.
>
> ■ The necessity of putting memorized words into meaningful use.

Another student, Dexter, was telling me about his unusual gift for learning isolated words.

'There are vocabularies for every page in the book,' he said, 'so I simply take the page and look at it.'

'You just look at it?'

'Oh, sure,' he replied. 'That's very easy. It's what I depend on. I don't honestly know that writing a word is going to mean that you will automatically recall it when you meet it on a page of small print.'

'And what happens after you have looked at the list?' I asked.

'Oh, I can often remember where it was on the page,' Dexter replied. 'But it's by no means an eidetic memory. That is, it's not a stable, sharp detailed picture, like some people get. And it doesn't last all that long. Nevertheless, the nouns and verbs are there pretty clearly.'

'For instance, you can say where it was on the page?'

'Either that, or I can say what it came before or after.'

'And right now, can you see anything that you studied last night?' I asked.

'Well, that depends,' Dexter replied. 'Sometimes you can, and sometimes you can't. Sometimes the word and its meaning stay, but the position on the page goes. Anyway, once you've gotten used to the word – once you've begun to use a word – once it has acquired a meaning . . .'

'Once you've attached it to experience rather than to . . .' I suggested.

'Exactly!' Dexter replied. 'Rather than to the position on the page! Then there's no real need to retain that visual memory, and as a consequence I think you forget it – deliberately, in a way. There's just no need for it – no room for it.'

'So this means that you do this sort of visual memorization as a temporary expedient to have these things available, so that when you have an opportunity to use them, then you *can* use them.'

'Right.'

'And then the visual part of it sort of drops off, like a rocket booster or something?'

'Yes. Yes, that's right.'

Comments

We learned from Derek how he works through assiduous shuffling and sorting of noun and verb forms, and through strenuous drill, in order to make the grammar of Finnish available to him. Now Dexter is telling us about an apparently less stressful way of being sure he can have access to another part of the language he is studying – its vocabulary. But both men seem to regard these resources as only temporary. In order to make them permanent, they must put them to some kind of use. Derek's 'imaginary brother' is only one example of how this can be done. Ann's Spanish vocabulary assignments are an example of what happens when this essential step is postponed too long, or omitted altogether.

Working with the ideas

1. Dexter does not really tell us very much about what goes on as he gazes at a vocabulary list. What questions might you want to ask him?
2. Dexter says that simply looking at the words produces better results for him than writing them out would. Is this consistent with your own experience?

4.2.5 Two ways of focusing on pronunciation

> ■ **Finding what one has been looking for.**
>
> ■ **DORA and DANIEL: 'Shadowing' a speaker.**

Finally, Derek turned to pronunciation. 'For me,' he remarked, 'mastering pronunciation is not anywhere near the conscious problem that mastering grammar and syntax is. I would say that most languages I have learned have been easy for an American to pronounce. That's true of Finnish, too. I suspect that it's more the rise and fall of the voice that marks the native speaker, and that's one thing I have never been conscious of learning.'

'You've used German and Russian in countries where they are spoken. Have you ever had any indications – probably indirect indications – as to whether your pronunciation is near native, or with a certain amount of accent, or . . . ?'

'Yes, I've had numerous indications. In Germany, people could not place me as an American. After any extended conversation, they could place me as a non-native German speaker.'

'Their initial reaction was that maybe you were a German from some other part of Germany . . .' I was reminded of Ann and Carla.

'Or a European, yes. But I do not have a trace of a distinctive American accent. And to some extent, the same thing happened in Russian.'

'Then you've been fairly successful with pronunciation.'

'I gather that I have. Of course one cannot listen constantly both to what people say and to how they say it, but I will interrupt my listening to content from time to time and say to myself, "Aha! So *that's* how they say it!" I'll be struck by the way a word or phrase is pronounced, and I'll try to imitate that way the next time I use the phrase.'

'You seem to be able to hear in your head today what you heard yesterday through your ears. You've still got the sound available.'

'Mhm. And another thing: I think reading aloud is excellent for developing pronunciation.'

Comments

Derek is probably better than most people at retaining the sounds of language. What was most striking to me, however, was his ability and willingness to shift his attention from *what* is being said to *how* it is said. Dora seems to have done the same sort of thing:

> When I was studying Spanish, I found that my teachers considered me to be an exceptional learner, even though I was receiving grades of B and C on grammar tests. My learning

took place in the classroom, speaking at every opportunity, and listening very attentively to the way the teacher pronounced each word. I would also carry on conversations with an imaginary native speaker. I could reproduce the way my teachers spoke, and 'hear' them in my head. I would also imagine myself speaking with that same accent. The more I practiced in this way, the better my pronunciation got. *I may have an innate ability to reproduce sounds, but it only came out when I focused on it.*

And Daniel, a high-school teacher of French, told me of one of his students who had an exquisitely good accent. 'The only thing he seems to do differently,' Daniel said, 'is that whatever I say in class, he's always repeating it quietly to himself as I talk.' The audibility of the student's shadowing of Daniel's pronunciation may have been the key. More important, I suspect, was the state of mind in which he did it – very much like Dora's as she echoed silently. Both Daniel's student and Dora were giving *close but unthinking attention* to what was coming into their ears.

Working with the ideas

1. Which aspects of Derek's study, if any, seem to you to have contributed significantly toward his 'interactive competence' (3.1.2)?
2. In what ways is Derek most like Ann? Like Bert? Like Carla? How is he most unlike them?
3. What did you find most surprising about Derek's way of learning languages?
4. What questions would you still like to ask him?

4.2.6 A TECHNIQUE: 'Shadowing' a news broadcast
Another technique from Derek

1. Listen to a newscast in your native language. Try repeating along with the speaker. Do this for at least two minutes.
   How did this 'shadowing' make you feel? How strenuous, or how relaxing, did you find it?
   After you had done it, how much did you remember of the content of what you had repeated?
2. Try doing the same thing in a language that is foreign to you. Don't let your mind stop to figure out or remember anything that you don't understand.
   How did this compare with 'shadowing' in your native language?
   How easy, or how hard, did you find it to keep from hanging up on the words and phrases that you didn't know?

4.3 Notes

1. The Cognitive Audio-Oral Bilingual method is an interesting attempt by Hector Hammerly of Simon Fraser University to combine the best (and get rid of the worst) in a number of well-known approaches to language learning. He describes his method in *An Integrated Theory of Language Teaching, and its Practical Consequences*, published in 1985 by Second Language Publications in Blaine, Washington.

2. John Rassias, a professor of French at Dartmouth College, gave an account of his system in *A Philosophy of Language Instruction*, the second edition of which was published privately in 1968.

Chapter Five

An Active Learner
Ed learning Korean, Rumanian and Swahili

Ed was a young officer who had served in Korea and Rumania, and had achieved high competence in the languages of both countries. At the time of our interview, he was doing exceedingly well as a student of Swahili. His manner as we talked was relaxed, happy, matter-of-fact. From our other contacts, I knew Ed to be an exceptionally active learner.

5.1 Pronunciation

Ed began by telling me how he worked on pronunciation. Much of what he said was surprising to me, even though I had watched him for several weeks in his study of Swahili.

5.1.1 Reading aloud to oneself

> ■ A technique that might be disastrous for some works well for others.

'In the first weeks of studying the language,' he began, 'I like to read it out loud, and get the sound.'

Just where Derek had ended his interview! But this still seemed to me like a violation of the principle that you can not say what you have not heard. 'By "reading out loud," do you mean that as soon as you learn how to read it off the page, you . . .?' I asked.

'As soon as I just learn how to pronounce it, yes.'

'And once you can pronounce it off the page, you like to read it aloud?'

'Yeah, I like to read it aloud, and I find that this persists even later, that it helps me in my own comprehension of reading anything, to read it aloud, hopefully with proper intonation and everything else. And once I know something about the language, I try to get the whole flow of the sentence. Sometimes I can understand the sentence without knowing all the words, for example.'

'You mean reading aloud, as contrasted with reading silently? There's something about that that makes it better?' I asked.

'Exactly! If I study at home, I can't study by just reading something silently. I'm not able to do that yet. I have to pronounce everything. I also think it helps you in memorizing words – memorizing vocabulary – to say things out loud. So that's one thing I know I definitely do do.'

'I noticed a few minutes ago, before we began the interview, you were reading some newspaper stories in Swahili, and you were reading them silently,' I pointed out.

'I didn't want to bother you,' Ed explained. 'If you hadn't been here, my inclination would have been to read them aloud. I remember, for example, I recently took the Rumanian test, and when I was given passages to translate, I read them aloud. I thought I would be able to translate them more easily if I read them aloud first.'

Comments

Ed's practice of reading aloud struck a chord with me. I had always found it very helpful to link what I was seeing with the things I was doing with my voice and tongue, and to link both of them with the sounds that came out. One year when I was in college, I lived in a suite with three occupants and two bedrooms. At the time, I was beginning the study of Russian. I knew from experience with Latin and German that I retained things much better if I studied them aloud. I had also discovered that it was easier to understand the grammatical structure of complicated sentences if I read them aloud. On this ground, I was allowed to have my own bedroom. Nevertheless, I know that many people are unlike Ed and me in this respect.

Working with the ideas

1. How many advantages does Ed list for reading aloud?
2. Which of these, if any, do you think would work for you?

5.1.2 EUGENE: Varieties of systematic repetition

- 'If I'm going to repeat something I've first got to know what it is.'

- Memorizing through repetition of understood material.

- Different media work better for different people.

Eugene was another of the interviewees about whose overall success I had no information. He did tell me that he had picked up a certain amount of German as a child. The language he was currently studying was totally unrelated to German.

'I cannot successfully reproduce meaningless noises,' Eugene told me. 'I've got to know what it is I'm trying to say. So I work a great deal on the written stuff, as a basis for learning to speak.'

'And this is what you've done in other languages?' I asked.

'Yes. Over a long period of time, I suppose you can absorb a language just by having somebody pound it into your head. But when you have a limited amount of time, *I* work best by understanding the language as it's written, and using that as a basis to go on.'

'Do you mean understanding in the sense of knowing what it means, or understanding in the sense of looking at it in written form, or . . .?'

'Both. Some people can listen to something said to them and reproduce it whether they understand it or not. I can't do that. You know, my mind rebels. And it's getting more rebellious as I get older.' Eugene laughed.

I laughed too. We were both over fifty years old.

'If I'm going to repeat something,' Eugene continued, 'I've first got to know what it *is*. I've got to know what this thing is supposed to mean, and break it up into its component parts.'

'Does this mean you make frequent use of English equivalents?' I asked.

'In the beginning, yes,' he replied.

'And then?' I asked.

'Well, if I have to memorize something,' Eugene replied, 'I just do it over and over and over.'

'And just what is it you do over and over?'

'Listening to the tapes. But then I write it out. I write it out so that I will know what it is I'm supposed to be saying . . . so that I can say it.'

'And having written it out in the language, then what do you do?'

'Then I memorize it. My test of whether I know it is my ability to reproduce it cold, on my own. "Can I do it right?" '

'Do it orally?'

'I do it first written, and then orally. If I try to rely on just listening and reading, it doesn't work.'

Comments

In his concern not to practice something until he 'knows what it *is*,' Eugene is consistent with the tenets of the CA-OB method (see 4.1.5).

On the surface, Eugene's technique is in striking contrast with Ed's: Eugene learned things by writing them out, while Ed learned them by reading or repeating aloud. Yet, on a more abstract level, I think I see some interesting similarities between the two men. Each was doing systematic repetition, each was working by himself at his own pace and each was using the medium that he found most congenial.

Working with the ideas

1. Overall, would you guess that Eugene was a more successful, or a less successful language learner than Ed? On what do you base your guess?
2. Aside from the matter of congeniality, what advantages can you see in Eugene's use of written repetitions? What disadvantages?
3. Are your own predilections more like Eugene's in this respect, or more like Ed's?

5.1.3 Building a set of auditory images

- 'After a while, I can tell if I'm saying it right.'
- Advantages and disadvantages of excellent pronunciation.
- The role of audio-tapes in Ed's study of pronunciation.
- Intense concentration.

'Any other thoughts on pronunciation?' I asked.

'I think pronunciation is extremely important,' Ed declared. 'In general, I put a great deal of effort on it in the first part of a language course. Actually, I've found my ability with pronunciation to be both an advantage and a handicap. It's an advantage because I think it makes me able to get the language better later, and people are better able to understand me. At the same time, it's always been a drawback, because I've frequently been mistaken in various countries for a native speaker.'

'And this creates expectations that you aren't able to live up to?'

'Well, yes, they assume that I know everything. You just say a couple of words, and people assume that you're a native speaker from someplace. They're not sure exactly where you come from. Maybe you've been living abroad for a long time. . .'

'Not from there, but at the same time, obviously not an American?'

'Or maybe you're not from there,' Ed answered, 'but you've been brought up in another country and your parents were from there.'

'You said a minute ago that you put quite a little effort into pronunciation. Effort in the sense of sitting and working with tapes by the hour? Effort in the sense of . . .?' I asked.

'I find tapes don't help me very much,' Ed replied. 'I find that listening to native speakers is better than tapes. I need to listen to a native speaker for an initial period to get the sounds of the language down. But after that, I find that just speaking aloud, just to myself, even with nobody correcting me, is enough. I can tell if I'm saying it properly or not. And if I'm not, I just listen more carefully next time.'

Serving as one's own critic for the improving of pronunciation again sounded to me like pulling oneself up by one's own bootstraps. It certainly violated conventional wisdom. 'Your ability to hear is enough ahead of your ability to produce so that practicing aloud doesn't get you into bad habits?' I asked.

'Well, *I* don't think it does,' he replied. 'In any case, I don't think correction is as important as just listening and trying to do it myself.' Maybe he was right, at least in his own case. If in fact he had often been mistaken for a native speaker, I could hardly quarrel with the results!

'It seems to be just the intensity of your concentration on that aspect of what the native speaker is doing,' I commented.

'Yes! Exactly!' Ed responded.

'When you do have that concentration, then you *are* almost performing the sentence along with the other person – with the teacher in this case.'

'Yeah, and when my mind works on vocalizing it inside, I hear the sound. I hear myself saying the sound.'

'While the teacher is saying it?' I asked.

'Almost as an echo of what the teacher is saying.'

'In your own voice, or in his voice?'

'I hear myself saying it, in my own voice.'

Comments

In describing his 'concentration,' Ed repeats almost word-for-word what Derek and Donna (4.1.2) and Dora and Daniel (4.2.5) said about 'shadowing' of native speakers. They give the language a steady kind of attention that is not broken by an anxiety to understand every word.

As a learner of various languages, I have found it useful to listen to tapes over and over, often just a word or a phrase at a time. When I do this, I focus my attention on one part after another. Like Ann and Bert, I can also profit from repeating a word many times after a native speaker, and having my pronunciation corrected. In both these ways, I can carefully build up my own auditory images of the vowels, consonants, rhythm and sentence melody. Ed clearly differs from us in these respects.

Working with the ideas

1. Ed seems to think that, even after having heard only a little of the language, he can establish a good pronunciation by reading aloud to himself. If he is right, how might this be possible?
2. In your own experience, have audio tapes been helpful in improving pronunciation?

5.1.4 A TECHNIQUE: Listening to one's own voice
A technique that Ed might have liked

One simple way to become more conscious of the sound of your own voice is to listen to its echo. You can do this conveniently if you sit facing into the corner of a plaster wall, or any other kind of corner that is close to your mouth and ear. Even an open book will do, but that requires you to use your hands.

Once you have arranged some sort of echo-source, read sentences or short texts aloud and just listen. One advantage of reading is that you can easily do the same thing over and over, concentrating on one feature at a time. Another advantage is that you can focus your attention on how you sound, rather than on what you are going to say next.

5.1.5 'Top-to-bottom' and 'bottom-to-top' in studying pronunciation

> ■ **Watching the speaker's mouth: a source of information, or a means to concentration?**
>
> ■ **The role of phonetic diagrams in Ed's learning of pronunciation.**

'I find it easier not to do just specific sounds, but to work on pronunciation in some kind of context,' Ed continued, 'a whole sentence if possible. That way I can get the whole flow of how the intonation goes, how the rhythm goes – the whole configuration all at once. I generally avoid getting too analytical and worrying about one sound at a time.'

'The whole utterance including its meaning, or just the way the whole utterance is pronounced?' I asked.

'No, not the meaning at first. In the early stages of learning a new language, I'd want to get at the sound first.'

'But the sound of whole phrases and sentences rather than individual vowels and consonants.'

'Yes. For one thing, I find it easier. For another, doing it that way is more accurate. I also find that explanations of sounds aren't very helpful.'

'Even explanations by experts?'

'That's right. They're more likely to be confusing than helpful. I find it very important to watch a native speaker's mouth, and try to do the same thing.'

I decided to interject a bit of my own interpretation. 'It's primarily a focus of attention, rather than anything else,' I opined.

Ed ignored my comment. 'I always feel it's something I want to get out of the way before going on to learn anything more,' he said, 'because I do in the end want to speak the language with a minimum of foreign accent.'

Comments

When Ed talked of 'watching the native speaker's mouth,' I didn't say anything. I had heard this idea before, from many successful learners of pronunciation. I had always scoffed at it, however. After all, most of the motions that cause differences in sound take place inside the mouth, or even in the throat, where no one can see them. Now I began to have second thoughts about my skepticism. The movements of the lips and some of the action of the tongue are visible from outside, of course. Even more important, perhaps, is the very act of fixing one's attention continuously on something outside one's control. That may have contributed to the concentration that Derek, Donna, Dora, Daniel and Ed have already described (5.1.3).

I have sometimes found both diagrams and explanations to be very helpful in my own language learning. I have also had the impression that many of my students in phonetics profited from them. Those aids represent a 'bottom-to-top' strategy for mastering pronunciation.

Ed apparently has no use for this strategy. His is just the opposite – one that is typical of 'acquisition' rather than of 'learning.' He prefers to start at the 'top,' with whole units, and work his way down. Although I have used the 'bottom-to-top' strategy myself and taught it to others, I have also worked from the 'top' down. I agree with Ed that this is the approach to choose if you are using only one. Readers should not reject diagrams and explanations if they find them helpful. But once having used these aids, I think most people will find it worthwhile to work with whole phrases the way Ed did.

Working with the ideas

1. Which strategy seems more natural to you for learning pronunciation, 'top-to-bottom' or 'bottom-to-top'?
2. How comfortable would you be pronouncing words and phrases without thinking about their meanings?

5.1.6 One emotional aspect of pronunciation

- ■ 'Hearing' what is going on in one's own head.
- ■ What is esthetically unwelcome is harder to assimilate.

'For me (and I really think this is idiosyncratic), I enjoy not having an accent,' Ed remarked. 'And I also find it's an impediment to my learning later if I feel that I'm not saying things properly.'

'An "impediment." Somehow or other, the new things don't fit you,' I suggested. 'They don't fit in quite so smoothly if you feel they're being said with an accent.'

'Yeah,' he replied, 'it just disturbs me somehow. I therefore feel that pronunciation is a priority, a thing to get out of the way.'

'New things – grammar or vocabulary or whatever – just aren't quite as welcome when they come in not sounding right?'

'To me, yes. I don't think it's necessarily this way for everybody. But even when I read things silently, I still *hear* it in my own mind, and I guess it bothers me if it doesn't sound right.'

'This is quite important to you.'

'Yes, because if I'm not comfortable with pronunciation, it's a big obstacle to working with new material. And come to think of it, that's interesting, because in English I *don't* hear myself when I read, unless I think it's something of literary value. Otherwise I usually speed-read. And the same was true when I was having to read and report on five Rumanian newspapers every morning. I didn't hear them, either!'

Comments

What Ed says here illustrates two principles:

- All the units of language come to us in a medium of speech or writing.
- What is esthetically unpleasant is harder to assimilate.

Vocabulary and grammar came to Ed via the words and sentences that he was pronouncing, whether externally or internally. If they continued to sound foreign, they would fit less easily into his internal resources for speaking Swahili. They would be an annoyance, a source of psychological allergy. Bert seemed not to have this difficulty. Both men illustrate both of the principles I have just listed. The difference between the two is simply that Bert did not mind sounding a bit foreign as long as he was easily understood, while Ed did mind.

Working with the ideas

1. What do you think Ed may have 'enjoyed' about not having a noticeable foreign accent?
2. How important would it be to you to minimize your accent in a new language?

5.2 Vocabulary and grammar

Ed had his own ways of actively approaching other aspects of the language as well.

5.2.1 'Learning' and 'acquisition' in the study of vocabulary

> ■ Playing to one's own natural strengths.
>
> ■ 'Get the structure first, then add vocabulary later as you need it.'
>
> ■ ELSA's friend: Get the vocabulary first!

'How do you go at the study of vocabulary?' I asked.

'Let me say first of all that I feel that sometimes an undue amount of attention is paid to vocabulary,' Ed began. 'And vocabulary in any language is overwhelming, because there are thousands and thousands of words that you could learn, and that's usually a matter of memorization, and I'm not very good at memorization, particularly if it's not in a very meaningful context. Some people do memorize very easily. My wife does, for example. Memorizing things is just not one of my strengths. So I don't worry about it.'

'You work with your strengths, and you avoid placing demands on yourself where you are weak.'

'Yes, and so I put more emphasis on structure than on vocabulary. I don't feel it's important to have a very large vocabulary while I'm learning a language. For me, what I'm trying to learn is the structural mechanics of the language, because the specific vocabulary that will be useful to me, whether at home, at work or wherever, I will inevitably learn.'

Comments

People vary greatly in the priority they give to vocabulary in a foreign language. Some experts say, 'If you understand the main features of the grammar, or if you at least have a good feel for them, then you can add vocabulary according to whatever situation you find yourself in. Therefore, focus first on grammar, within whatever small vocabulary is convenient.' Other experts say, 'If you understand the main words in a sentence, you can usually get a good idea of its meaning. And if you understand what a sentence means, you can gradually come to see how its grammar works. Therefore, focus first on recognizing plenty of words.'

The first of these two positions is the one that fits in with academic 'learning,' as we used that term in 1.1.2. The second is more consistent with an attempt to 'acquire' a new language more or less in the way that one acquired one's first language. Ed here echoes the 'learning' position for grammar and vocabulary. This is especially interesting because, as we saw in 5.1.5, he seems to prefer to 'acquire' pronunciation.

Elsa, a German-speaking friend, tells me of an American who as an adult learned to speak quite good German. His way? He began by selecting one situation at a time, and memorizing as many nouns as he could that had to do with it. Then he would put himself into that situation and try to talk with people. An interesting combination of 'learning' and 'acquisition' techniques! And an interesting progression from temporary 'stockpiling' to permanence!

Perhaps the most important point that Ed makes in this segment is a very general one: he builds his learning style around his strengths, and does not worry about his weaknesses.

Working with the ideas

1. Do you find Ed's reasons for emphasizing grammar at the beginning of his course convincing? Why, or why not?
2. What are your own strengths in this regard?
3. Which do you think would be best for you to emphasize at the beginning of a new language, vocabulary or grammar? To what extent is your answer based on experience? To what extent is it based on esthetic preferences?

5.2.2 Terminology is not essential to 'understanding' grammar

---

- ■ Technical vs practical knowledge of a language.

- ■ Concern about incompleteness of 'learning' may become an impediment to 'acquisition.'

'And that brings us to structure,' I said.

'I think that once I get overseas, the thing that helps the most, more than a lot of vocabulary, is the basic structure,' Ed said.

'The grammar, that kind of thing?' I asked.

'I'm talking about a real ability to manipulate the grammar, not necessarily an analytical approach to the grammar,' Ed replied. 'The technical part doesn't concern me so much as my capacity as a user of the language. I mean, when I sit down and read a sentence, I feel that I really want to understand how to take it apart, and how it's put together, and why,' He explained. 'I feel uncomfortable if I'm not able to understand what all the little particles are, and how they fit in. I don't read everything that way every time, but I don't feel comfortable in reading something unless I know that I *can* understand those things if I stop and ask myself.'

I thought I saw what Ed was getting at. 'When you talk about "taking apart," you mean that if you learn a new dialog or something, you go through it and either have somebody give you a grammatical term such as "object pronoun" or whatever, or at least so that you feel that you know what that thing is doing there, and what would happen if something else were put in its place. You want some way of accounting for that. Is this getting at what you mean?' I asked.

'Yes,' Ed replied, 'I don't care if you call it the "object pronoun" or whatever – the jargon of it doesn't matter – but what I'm interested in is the function: why is that particle inserted into the middle of that word? What did it do? What does it refer to? How will it change if the word to which it refers changes? What happens then? That sort of thing.'

'"What will happen?" rather than "What do you call it?"?'

'Exactly. All I want to do is be able to use it. But I find it helps me be able to do that later on if I have some of these structural things very clearly in my mind – subconsciously. I don't want to think about them as I go along trying to learn the language. But I find it impedes me if I try to learn something by doing an analysis. That makes it more difficult. I'd rather learn something new by sheer mimicry and memorization.'

Comments

Small children are not uncomfortable if they do not understand all the prefixes, suffixes and little connecting words of their language. Ed says he is. Again, Ed is emphasizing 'learning' rather than 'acquisition' (see 1.1.2).

On the other hand, Ed is not really concerned with being able to recite rules or to learn technical terminology. He only wants to know, 'If I make a change here in the sentence, what will it require me to do in the rest of the sentence?' or 'If I hear this little word or this prefix, what does it lead me to expect somewhere else?' In my experience, this is a distinction of the greatest practical importance to anyone learning a new language. I have watched many English-speaking students of foreign languages over the years. Too many of them were anxious because they had never learned to pin labels like 'participle' onto the words in English sentences. Yet none of them would have had any difficulty in saying, 'I saw Frank crossing the street' and all would have known that the person who was crossing the street was Frank, and not the speaker. This is the kind of practical knowledge that Ed was talking about.

Working with the ideas

1. How comfortable are you in just 'getting the gist' of something you are reading, even if you do not understand the details?
2. How easy do you find it to learn and use rules, either in your own language or in a foreign language?

5.2.3 'Top-to-bottom' and 'bottom-to-top' in studying vocabulary

---

- Reading for gist.

- Alternation between 'upward' and 'downward' work with language.

'This, then, is how you most profitably go at new languages, as you say, getting an excellent feel for the structure within a small vocabulary.'

'Yeah, I think it's very important to get that type of thing. But during the presentation of new material, I sometimes find it good to just learn something – memorize it or whatever – and only then to break it down, to look at it and find out what has happened: *How* has this been put together? *Why* has it been put together this way? To ask and answer questions like that, and then forget about it.'

'A very practical attitude toward grammar, then.'

'I'd say so. Of course, I do need something to analyze – some kind of meaningful text. I don't think you can begin by saying "This is a particle, and you combine this particle with something else" and so on. You have to begin with something that makes some kind of sense to you. But then I'll leave it alone. I don't want to persist, and continue to look at each sentence analytically.'

'The time for taking things apart has passed.'

'That's right. I want to go ahead and speak the language, and listen to the language, and comprehend it. However, I find that, particularly when it comes to unfamiliar material, if I open up a book that I've never seen before, where I have a lack of vocabulary, I find it very easy to read it and get a general idea of what it's about.'

'Drawing on your small vocabulary and your feel for the structure?'

'Yes. Yes, and then if I'm interested, I can get a dictionary and look up the words. On the other hand, if you know all the vocabulary but don't know the syntax, then you can sort of figure out what's being said, but you don't really understand it.'

'You guess,' I said.

'Yeah, you figure it out as you go along, and I don't find that very satisfactory.'

Comments

Ed rejects the 'bottom-to-top' approach (see 1.2.1) of starting with words and prefixes and building them into sentences. He wants to start at the 'top,' with sentences and longer samples of language that will be meaningful to him. On the other hand, he does not want to stay very long at the 'top.' He *can* 'get the gist,' but he prefers not to. He would rather work immediately 'downward,' turning his attention to the words and prefixes that allow the samples to have their meanings.

But having once moved to the 'bottom' and discovered what the prefixes and little words are doing in the sentence, Ed does not want to stay there. He is ready to go back to the next meaningful whole sentence of whatever he is reading or listening to. I suspect that this regular, almost rhythmic alternation between 'top' and 'bottom' is a large part of the secret of Ed's success.

Working with the ideas

1. What apparent inconsistencies have we discovered in what Ed has told us up to this point in his interview?
2. On the basis of what you have learned so far about Ed, how is he most unlike Derek? How is he most similar to Carla?

5.2.4 Resources: rules, regularities and routines

■ The importance of keeping actively involved.

■ 'Monitoring.'

'If you were listening while somebody was giving a public address,' I speculated, 'you might listen for fifteen minutes at a time. But in a situation where you can interrupt, to restate what a person has said, to answer their question, to complete their sentence or whatever, I'd guess that you find that even better. You can overtly participate either by answering their question or by restating what the other person has said, or by completing their sentence.'

'Well, as a learning technique, yes,' Ed replied. 'For me, it's very important to be active as much of the time as possible. I can't learn very much passively. There are times when I can sit and listen to something for long periods of time, but I find that sort of relaxing, rather than instructive.'

'Not really a part of your language study.'

'No, I don't feel I'm actively learning a thing then. The only thing I learn, sometimes, in that passive situation, is new vocabulary. I get the gist of a story, and the meaning of certain words becomes very clear just by context. But it doesn't help very much to fix the grammar in my mind. It doesn't allow me to manipulate a thing.'

'Whereas the active kind of participation you were talking about does help you with the grammar and so forth?'

'I feel that way. I feel that way. I feel it's very important for me to say something properly.'

Comments

The only thing Ed thinks he learns passively is vocabulary, and we have already seen that he does not attach much value to that. He wants to 'manipulate' the structures of his sentences, and for that he feels the need to be active. Moreover, he wants be active in a meaningful situation. That way, all the elements of sight and sound and feeling and purpose and emotion and all the rest are stored in his mind along with the sentences and the changes he makes in them.

In 5.1.6, Ed said he does not like to pronounce things wrong. Now he tells us that he feels the same about grammar. In both these areas, he listens to himself (or he reads what he is writing). As he listens (or reads), he *compares* two things: one is the Swahili or Rumanian or Korean sentence he is hearing (or reading) at the moment; the other is an equivalent sentence that his mind is generating.

But where is Ed 'generating' his sentence from? He is actually drawing on a combination of at least three kinds of *resources*. Some of these resources are

(1) explicit *rules*. Rules are the resources that language learners and many language teachers are most likely to think about: 'Place the indirect object before the direct object' and so on. Other important resources, however, are (2) *remembered* sentences or sentence fragments: 'Do you know what time the shops close?' Still others are drawn from Ed's experiences with (3) *regularities* – experiences with how a change at one point in a sentence will require a change somewhere else (5.2.2). Carroll was also talking about this kind of thing (see 1.1.1).

The distinctions among *rules*, *regularities* and *remembered material* need a bit of illustration. Imagine a person who had frequently heard the English sentence *I don't care*, but did not know the rules for forming it, and who also lacked much experience with English. Operating with *remembered material*, such a person might produce the sentence *I don't care* correctly, but might still say *I no see it*, or *I not understand*.

The *relationship* between the sentences:

I see it   I don't see it

is the same as the *relationship* between:

We know them   We don't know them

A person who has somehow responded to this *regularity* – this sameness of relationship, and who is already able to say:

They have it

will also be able to say:

They don't have it.

instead of *They no have it*, *They have it not*, etc.

A *rule*, as I am using that term here, is a formulation in words:

In order to form a negative statement in the present tense, place the auxiliary verb *do* after the subject, add the word *not*, and then follow the rule for contracting those two words.

In order to make use of such a rule, one would first have to remember it, then recognize that one is dealing with a present-tense sentence that should be negative, and then go on and apply the rule one step at a time. This can be a time-consuming process. Ed is a person who is often able to go through this process rapidly enough so that it does not interfere with communication. Carla apparently found this kind of thing prohibitively cumbersome, if not impossible.

We all do this kind of comparing constantly in our native language, using a combination of resources. That is how we catch and correct ourselves when we say something we did not mean, or when we say (or write) something that simply is not said in our language: 'I arrived on – I mean *at* – the airport at 10:15.' This process of listening to (or reading) our own output and checking it is sometimes called 'monitoring.' Monitoring is also important in foreign languages. Ed is saying that he is eager to build up a full range of resources for monitoring his Swahili.

(Note: Some writers use the term 'monitoring' only or primarily when the resources being drawn on are rules.)

Working with the ideas

1. During the next twenty-four hours, listen for examples of self-correction (or of uncorrected errors) by native speakers on the radio or on television. (These are surprisingly frequent in newscasts, interviews and other unrehearsed programs.)
2. Up to this point, what do we know about Ed's ways of assembling resources for monitoring his Swahili?
3. What kinds of resources did Carla draw on for monitoring her German? What resources did Derek use?

5.2.5 *Using drills to promote spontaneity*

- Ed's overall approach.

- Relationship among rules, regularities and remembered fragments.

I decided to try to summarize what I thought Ed had been saying about his style of learning. 'So if you were taking up a new language,' I began, 'if you were studying Tamil, for example – your strategy would be to first of all get comfortable with the pronunciation by concentrating on the sounds of phrases and sentences.'

'Mhm,' he replied.

'And having once gotten comfortable with that – once your ear was good enough to correct your tongue, so to speak – you would then go on practicing by yourself.'

'Yeah. There's always a gap, though. I think I'm able to hear better than I'm able to produce. But it gets better. The gap decreases over time.'

'You'd practice by yourself until you got comfortable with the sounds, and with your own inaudible pronunciation of them. That would be your first major goal.'

'Mhm.'

'And having reached that goal, then you'd go at short, meaningful texts, and take them apart to see how the parts relate to each other – even the very smallest parts. Then you'd kind of forget about that, or let it kind of sink in, outside of the focus of your concentration, and you'd go on pretty much communicating, reading interesting things, or whatever it might be, and letting the vocabulary take care of itself by circumlocution or otherwise. And just as your ear was better than your tongue, so your understanding of grammar is better than your ability to produce it spontaneously. And as time goes on, more and more things come out right spontaneously.'

'Yes, that's a good overall summary,' Ed replied. 'However, in learning grammar, I don't think it's adequate just to have something presented in a text, analyze it and from that figure out the grammar. That's all right as far as it goes. But I think after having done that, it's very important to drill. Some things need more drill, some less.' Ed's voice became more emphatic. 'But with the points that are difficult,' he went on, 'I think it's very important for me to drill them until they do become spontaneous, so that I don't have to think about them when I'm speaking!'

Comments

Like Derek and Bert, Ed is quite insistent on the value of what he calls 'drill.' Here he mentions 'figuring out the grammar.' We have already seen (5.2.4) that for Ed this does not necessarily mean memorizing formal rules or applying academic terminology. It does, however, mean reaching some sort of understanding that could be put into words if he wanted to. So 'figuring out the grammar' adds at least temporarily to the 'rules' that Ed has available to him (see 5.2.4).

What Ed seems to be telling us here is that rules are not enough. There may be two reasons why he feels this way. One is that it takes time to utilize rules in speaking or writing. The other is that a rule which is not tied in with other kinds of resources is quickly lost. The most conspicuous feature of drills is that they are repetitious. Ed practices the same sentences over and over, and (as we saw in 5.2.4) he is required to notice and respond to regularities in the relationships among them. These sentences and these regularities thus become integrated into the network of resources out of which Ed can produce and monitor his Swahili. All these kinds of resources are linked to one another, and so they help to retain one another in Ed's memory. The good thing about regularities and remembered fragments is that they operate more quickly than rules.

Working with the ideas

1. In what ways is this summary of Ed's learning strategy similar to Derek's? In what ways is it different?
2. In what ways would you find Ed's strategy easy to follow? In what ways would you find it most alien from how your mind works?

5.2.6 Structured conversation as an alternative to drill

> ■ **Mastery of one point before moving to the next.**
>
> ■ **Drill as a means of resolving uncertainty and alleviating frustration.**

'And that's where ordinary drills come in?' I asked.

'Yes. For me, I find it very useful to be drilled. For instance, I think I would have had less trouble with Swahili concords if I'd been drilled in them more.' (Since I was the supervisor of the Swahili course, this observation of Ed's was of particular interest to me!)

'In your way of going at things,' I responded, 'the time for drill on a point is very soon after you first understand it.' Ed nodded. 'Right after you've understood something out of a connected context, and taken the context apart. So, instead of having to go on the next day and . . .'

'And learn something else,' Ed supplied.

'Instead of that,' I went on, 'or instead of having to go on the next day and rediscover that same thing by taking another text apart, time and effort can be saved, in your experience, by putting in a drill fairly soon after that first time.'

'Time, effort and *frustration*!' he said firmly. 'I think when you've learned a point of grammar or whatever, it's very important that you use that point properly *from then on*, including being corrected by the teacher. Of course, I suppose if you're corrected *too* often, it can damage your confidence, but I think it's possible to do structured conversation which centers around a particular grammar point or a set of vocabulary items or whatever, such that in the course of the conversation you can eliminate a problem, a shortcoming, a source of annoyance.'

'You'd really like to have more drill,' I commented.

'Well, of course one doesn't always have to exercise by using only the simplest, most mechanical types of drill. There are ways of doing it in an interesting manner without making it painful. But, however it's done, I want to get each point down thoroughly before moving on to another one.'

Comments

We saw in 5.2.5 that rules by themselves quickly evaporate. If Ed is to tie a rule in with the corresponding regularities and remembered fragments, he must do so quickly, while it is still available. Not to do so constitutes a waste of the time and intellectual energy that he had put into arriving at the rule (or into understanding it when somebody gave it to him). This, I suspect, is the basis for the annoyance and frustration that Ed expresses here.

Drills are often dry and mechanical, but for Ed these are not their most important features. They are only means to an end: they are ways of providing concentrated exposure to regularities and to specific bits of language. When he mentions 'structured conversation,' Ed is saying that a skillful teacher or learner can attain this end by another means: by planning and guiding real conversations.[1] We will see that Gwen, who is skillful both as a teacher and as a learner, makes frequent use of this device. For example, one can practice comparative forms of adjectives by talking about real people or people out of stories, saying who is older, taller and so forth.

Working with the ideas

1. Have someone tell you a set of unfamiliar street directions. Try to remember just the words.

Listen to another set of directions, to a different destination. Try to visualize them as you listen.

Listen to a third set. As you listen, try to draw a simple map that corresponds to them.

Which set of directions are you most likely to be able to remember twenty-four hours later?

2. One thing that learners and teachers of English have to deal with is the contrast among the forms of verbs: *break*, *broke*, *broken*, for example. How could one structure a conversation so as to provide concentrated practice on this part of the language?

5.2.7 The importance of assimilation

> ■ **Short interval between uncertainty and explanation, and between explanation and examples.**
>
> ■ **Remembering things by writing them out.**

'In this assimilation process you speak of,' I said, 'you get something new, and eventually it becomes part of you so that it automatically comes out right . . .'

'That's correct. It becomes a part of me – a part of the resources I have at my command.'

'But in between, there's this assimilation process, and if the assimilation process is unnecessarily protracted because there isn't the needed drill or structured conversation or whatever, and the assimilation process has not taken place, then it kind of rankles,' I ventured.

I was not prepared for the strength of Ed's response. 'That's right! Exactly! Exactly!' Ed replied. 'And one thing that helps me get it into my mind is writing it down,' he added.

'Your policy is therefore "Let's get this assimilation process *over* with!"'

'Yes. In sum, ideally I like to be presented with a thing, learn it intellectually, then assimilate it, and then go on to something new.'

'And the assimilation process for you involves . . .'

'Drill!'

'Drill. Working at the point systematically, and fairly concentrated in time. Instead of having an example of it today, and then maybe another example of it the day after tomorrow, you'd like to have a couple of dozen examples within a five-minute period so that you can work with it.'

'I want those several dozen examples immediately!' Ed replied with some animation. 'But I also want future examples. Then, two weeks later, I won't need any more examples. All I'll need is to have someone point out when I've made a mistake, and I'll be able to correct myself!'

Comments:

I am sure that Ed had never heard of the 'CA-OB method.' What he says here is, however, very close to a statement from its manual: 'Initially slow, conscious responses are speeded up through increasingly faster and more meaningful practice until the responses can be generated largely unconsciously, at normal speed, with attention to meaning.'[2]

Writing things out is an old-fashioned device that I had always looked down on because I don't use it much myself. Oral practice has been much more efficient for me. The Audio-Lingual approach, under which I had much of my early training, also tended to minimize the importance of writing. Yet the act of writing does add visual and muscular items to the network of resources that Ed will have available in his memory. He reminds us that for some people this set of items may be much more powerful (and much less expensive in time and energy) than for others.

Working with the ideas

1. Reading things aloud and writing them out are two ways of making them more available in the future. Which has seemed more effective for you?
2. In what ways was Ed building his 'interactive competence' and not just his 'linguistic competence' (see 3.1.2)?

5.3 Observing one's own mental activity

Ed was also keenly aware of what was going on inside his own head.

5.3.1 'Shadowing' grammar as well as pronunciation

> ■ Forming, testing and using hypotheses about the relationship between forms and meanings.
>
> ■ Deliberate echoing or copying of an interlocutor's structures.

'One of the things that I like to do when I can concentrate,' Ed remarked, 'is to just simply listen to the teacher very carefully, and sort of mimic.'

'Mimic silently?' I asked. It seemed to me that audible mimicry would have been rude. But Ed was more subtle in how he did it.

'No,' he replied, 'I mean mimic out loud, perhaps in reply to a question. Or not even a question, but in a conversation. I let him say something, and then I just say the same thing back, changing it slightly so that it's suitable as a continuation of the conversation.'

When Ed spoke of 'mimicry', I had assumed he was talking about pronunciation again. Now I realized he was talking mainly about grammar.

'But what I'm really trying to do,' he continued, 'is to use long sentences, long phrases, trying to expand my memory in the language, and particularly paying attention to getting all those little particles and such things. Not just trying to remember the basic part of the sentence, but trying to remember how it was that he put all those things together in a way that sounds right.'

'So when you say "mimicry", you're really talking about a kind of echoing activity, where you still have these things in some kind of immediate memory. You have them temporarily available, so now you're using them yourself . . .'

'Using them immediately!'

'Immediately. And this helps.'

'Yeah, I find that sometimes I even go so far as to interrupt the teacher.'

'In order to have a chance to . . .?' I inquired.

'To finish the sentence.'

'To finish it as you thought he was going to finish it?'

'Well, I don't care how he was going to finish it. I'm using it in my mind even while he's speaking, and I let him go along until I maybe have a beautiful ending for the sentence, and then I go ahead and finish it. Maybe I don't finish it the way he would have.'

'Then you're really involved in the sentence even as it's being spoken by the other person.'

'Yes, and this requires a fair amount of concentration. I do find sometimes that my mind wanders. But maybe 80 per cent of the time, I'm able to maintain that kind of concentration.'

Comments

Once more we hear of the value of concentration. This time, however, concentration is not simply a matter of steady, non-critical attention. Ed is giving quick *scrutiny* to each fragment as it goes past. He is also trying to *remember* things that he has not yet mastered. Shadowing grammar is more demanding than merely shadowing pronunciation.

But Ed was doing more than shadowing the grammar of what he was hearing. He was also following its *meaning*. That is to say, he was constructing in his head a continuous flow of mental images that fitted the flow of words. On top of that, he was *testing and using* those mental images by at least silently finishing the other person's sentence ahead of him. The relaxed and casual way in which Ed talked about it made it sound easy. I still considered it a remarkable performance, however.

Working with the ideas

1. From among Ann, Bert, Carla and Derek, which do you think would be most likely to do what Ed has described in this segment? What makes you think so?
2. In the comments on 5.2.4 we mentioned three kinds of resource on which

people may draw for monitoring their own speech or writing.

Which resources did Ed depend on while shadowing the grammar of what he was hearing or reading?

Which kinds of resources do you suppose he used most when he completed the other speaker's sentences?

5.3.2 The conditions for 'monitoring'

> ■ Relationship between 'learned' material and the
>   process of 'acquisition.'
>
> ■ Balancing the need for fluency and the need for
>   accuracy.

Ed again changed the subject. 'One interesting thing I've noticed,' he said, 'is that I frequently make mistakes in saying something, even though I know the proper form. When I do my homework assignments in Swahili, I sometimes have to write compositions at home, and rarely in those compositions will I make more than three or four mistakes in a 300–400-word composition.'

Because I was connected with the Swahili course, I knew that Ed's evaluation of his own writing was accurate. 'One factor is that I'm sitting quietly thinking about it as I'm writing it down,' Ed continued. 'But something happens also when I actually have to produce it on paper. I mean that in class I'm somehow not hearing myself correctly. I make mistakes in class when I know the correct form, consciously, and if I'm stopped and asked about it I will most of the time produce the correct form. It's not a question of not knowing it. But somehow or other, when I just speak quickly in class, apparently I don't say the right thing – leaving out a particle, or putting in a wrong prefix, or something like that. I don't make those mistakes when I write on paper. I don't know why.'

Ed seemed genuinely surprised at this. I was surprised that he was surprised. This however was not the time for me to inject my views into the conversation. 'You're saying that, given the same subject matter, you make many fewer mistakes when you're by yourself, at leisure, writing things out,' I said by way of summary.

'Yes,' he answered, 'when I write it, I have to sit there and look at each letter and consider what it should be, and when I really have to think about each little segment, I rarely make a mistake. So I think I've pretty well assimilated the rules. The trouble is in producing them rapidly and spontaneously, without thinking about it. Sometimes I'm a little bit sloppy about doing this.'

'Do you think it's simply a matter of having time when you're writing things out, or do you think there's more to it that that?' I asked. I was wondering whether he would say that it was also a matter of focusing his attention on form instead of on meaning.

'I think I haven't yet made the transition to where I can simultaneously think in and use the language. I'm sure it'll happen within six months of the time I get to Dar es Salaam.'

'Think and talk simultaneously.'

'Yes. Of course I don't mean perfectly simultaneously. I mean almost simultaneously. Right now, I'm doing a lot of translating in my mind. When a subject is very interesting in a conversation, the production gets ahead of the analysis – or of the mental translation. Then I'm more interested in communicating something, even imperfectly, than I am in thinking about each little detail.' Yes, here was the question of where attention was focused.

Ed continued. 'So fluency is at the expense of accuracy,' he said. 'That doesn't bother me very much, because I've found with other languages that when I get to a place where I hear the language being used a lot, I just simply start listening to native speakers and imitating them – mimicking them – and so without making any great effort to eradicate the specific mistakes, I will eradicate them.'

'They just go away?'

'They just go away. Right now, I'm at a stage where I need to pay more attention to each one of those little details of grammar. It's not that I don't know them in an academic sense, but I haven't fully assimilated them so that they're just a normal part of the way I use the language.'

'To put it another way,' I suggested, 'even when you're at your most fluent, and most involved in the conversation, there are certain things that you don't make mistakes on.'

'That's right.'

'There are, on the other hand, some things that you make mistakes on when you're being fluent and concentrating on the subject matter.'

'Right.'

'And these are mistakes that you wouldn't make if you were writing the same subject matter. And what I think you're saying is that, as you get into the country and talk with people, or as time goes by, this gradually gets transferred from one of those categories to the other.'

'I think that's the way it happens,' Ed replied. 'I do know I certainly make fewer mistakes now than I did two months ago, and there are certain things that were problems that are no longer real problems – concord, for instance.'

Comments

'Monitoring' (see 5.2.4) is easier when we have plenty of time, and when our attention is on *how* we are saying or writing something rather than *what*. This has been documented by research,[3] but it is also common experience. That was why I was surprised that Ed thought this aspect of his experience was remarkable. I was also interested to hear Ed use an emotionally loaded word like 'sloppy' to describe his occasional lapses in monitoring.

Yet I think it would be inaccurate to say that correctness depends *only* on these two factors of time and attention. I have seen instances where a person who was excited about what he was saying actually spoke not only faster, but also more correctly than usual. There are, after all, two ways of producing correct language. The more obvious of the two is to monitor what one is saying and make corrections. Less obvious but more important, one can also draw on resources in such a way as to produce sentences that need no correction in the first place. Perhaps (and this is only a guess) certain kinds of excitement activate those resources more fully than ordinary, careful classroom recitation does.

Some of any speaker's resources have come through a process of deliberate, conscious 'learning.' Other resources have come through a process that we called 'acquisition' (see 1.1.2). The former can be built rather quickly, but they also tend to be forgotten quickly. Even when they have not been forgotten, it generally takes more time and effort to mobilize them when we need them. 'Acquisition' builds resources more gradually and more slowly. Once such resources are in place, however, they tend to stay in place, and to be available with little delay or effort.

Ed's learning sometimes sounds like the sequence outlined for the Natural Approach (see 1.1.4). At other times, it is more consistent with the CA-OB sequence (see 4.1.5). Here Ed seems to be saying that as time goes on, certain points of grammar get transferred from the 'learned' to the 'acquired' category. Perhaps what he means is that at first he had to recall and use a rule in order to avoid a certain kind of error. Later, after he had accumulated more sentences and sentence-fragments, and after he had had more experience with how a change at one point requires changes at other points, he found himself depending more on these latter resources, and less on rules.

Working with the ideas

1. One day recently I heard myself say that something had 'slidden' onto the floor. What kind of resources were behind that incorrect word?
2. I of course immediately corrected myself and said 'slid.' How can one account for this correction in terms of the comments on 5.2.4?

5.3.3 Fluctuating energy levels

> ■ **Even outstanding learners are human!**

Ed was silent for a moment, and then came up with a final comment. 'Another thing – another observation I've made,' he said, 'at the beginning of a new language course, I have a lot more energy for studying – for doing things at home. But after a certain period, it becomes boring. I just don't have the incentive. It's not that I think I can't absorb any more. This feeling comes and goes, usually in cycles.'

'Maybe in the first few weeks, these cycles are more or less cancelled out by the newness, the reservoir of initial enthusiasm?' I wondered.

'Whatever the reason, in the first weeks I feel no strain at all in continuing my study after I get home.'

'But it goes in cycles.'

'Yes. Two weeks ago, for instance, I absolutely could not do anything outside of class, and right now I can. I even ask the teacher for something to do because I feel I want to continue doing something. In addition to knowing that it's good to keep working, I *feel* like doing it now.'

'You've noticed these ups and downs in other language courses.'

'Mhm.'

Comments

I found it reassuring to hear that even a highly talented learner like Ed sometimes had his ups and downs.

Working with the ideas

1. Have you noticed similar cycles in your own level of energy and enthusiasm for academic study?
2. Have these fluctuations been more noticeable in subjects that you found easy and interesting, or in those that were difficult and dull for you?
3. How does Ed's interview fit the lists provided by Carroll (see 1.1.1) and Omaggio (see 1.2.6)?
4. What questions would you still like to ask Ed?

5.4 Notes

1. Structured communication tasks are described in many books on language teaching, including the one by Heidi Dulay, Marina Burt and Stephen D. Krashen (Chapter 1, note 3), Mario Rinvolucri's *Grammar Games* (Cambridge University Press, 1984) and Gertrude Moskowitz' *Caring and Sharing in the Foreign Language Class* (Newbury House, 1978). A book that is aimed at learners rather than teachers is *Becoming Bilingual*, by Donald N. Larson and William A. Smalley. It was published in 1984 by the University Press of America, in Lanham, Maryland.
2. Hector Hammerly (see Chapter 4, note 1), p. 83.
3. On p. 30 of their book (see Chapter 1, note 7), Krashen and Terrell talk about the conditions for monitoring. Stephen Krashen has more to say on the subject in *Principles and Practice in Second Language Acquisition* (Pergamon Press, 1982).

Chapter Six

A Deliberate Learner
Frieda learning Arabic and Hebrew

Frieda was a young woman who had been highly successful in her study of Arabic, first in a university and then in the Arab world. Her experience with that language had led her to take a course in Hebrew, which is related to it linguistically. She was disappointed, however.

6.1 Texts and grammar

For me, Frieda's most noticeable characteristic was the deliberateness with which she undertook everything, including the learning of dialogs and the study of grammar.

6.1.1 Reading before speaking

> - **Discomfort at having to repeat aloud before seeing.**
> - **Possible effects of teacher's personal style.**

'I'm not one of those people who are capable of absorbing a language by the Audio-Lingual method,' she began. 'I had one failure in language learning. I took a course in Hebrew. We had no books *per se*. The teacher said we could buy the textbook, but she herself never opened a book in class. She would shout a dialog at us, and we had to repeat it after her again and again and again until . . .'

'Without seeing it?' I asked.

'Without seeing it. I was miserable. I couldn't say a thing. I couldn't remember what she was saying. And in each lesson, she would introduce a new dialog, and I didn't know what was going on. Then finally, I got wise and went out and bought a copy of the book, and I studied all the lessons. They were all done in roman transcription, so that people could learn them very quickly. Then I got one step ahead of her, and learned the next dialog.'

'So you were able to shout them back!'

'So I was able to shout them back! She was absolutely amazed. I had been so stupid . . .!'

'And suddenly you had become so bright!'

'Yeah. And so I found that one important thing was to be able to see what I had in front of me.'

Comments

Frieda wants to see things before she tries to say them. In this respect, she vindicates the CA-OB outline (see 4.1.5). On the other hand, she seems to be the exact opposite of Ann, who told us she did most of her learning through her ears (see 1.1.1).

The Hebrew teacher's method posed a twofold obstacle to Frieda's learning. Technically, it demanded that Frieda perform well in an area where she was weak, and it did not provide her with an opportunity to exploit her strengths. Frieda solved this problem by going out and buying herself a book. The other problem was more subtle: Frieda apparently did not like the teacher's manner. In words like 'shout' and 'stupid' we can catch some echoes of the feelings she must have had in the class. So, although she soon began to amaze the teacher with her performance in class, Frieda still considered the course to have been 'a failure.'

Working with the ideas

1. In the above comments, I mentioned two words which conveyed some of Frieda's negative feelings about the Hebrew course. What other evidences can you find?
2. Do you think it was ethical of Frieda to look ahead and memorize the next dialog from the roman transcription? If it was ethical, do you think it was wise? Why, or why not?

6.1.2 The importance of personal involvement

> ■ Psychological involvement.
>
> ■ Total Physical Response (Asher).

'In Arabic, after basic work on pronunciation, we started with dialogs,' Frieda continued. 'For me it was more than an academic exercise. It was very important for me, as a person, to be able to know how to say, "I'm going to the university," or "I'm studying my Arabic." It was more than just an academic exercise! I took it very personally, even though we were just working with controlled basic texts, with a controlled amount of vocabulary and structures. For me it was very important that *I* be able to communicate it in a genuine way!'

'Wait a minute!' I interrupted. 'It sounds like there's something very important here. It was not only a matter of being able to recite it, to perform it in class. Is that what you're saying?'

'No, not just in class.'

'It was that,' I continued, 'but it was also that you made this a part of yourself, you really put your whole self into it!'

'Oh, yes! Your whole self has to be in it!' Frieda replied. 'I would speak to myself in Arabic at home, you know. If I knew how to say to myself "I have to look for my hairbrush," I would say it. My mother would think I was crazy, but . . .'

'The textbook, then, kind of preordained what it was that you were going to *terribly* want to learn the next day. And then you went ahead and *terribly* wanted to learn it. Was that . . . ?'

'That was it! But I also added to it from the outside.'

'You practiced talking to yourself?'

'Talking to myself, and there are always native speakers that you can use as informants, or people, you know, that are on other levels. For example, if for some particular reason I wanted to say "I am going downtown," I would find anybody – anybody – who could tell me how to say that, and I would practice it until it made sense.'

'This might be a sentence that hadn't come up in the book yet?'

'No, it hadn't necessarily come up in the book.'

Comments

When I said 'you went ahead and terribly wanted to learn it,' I was thinking of Derek's maxim: 'If you can't learn to say what you want to say, then learn to want to say what you can say!' (see 4.2.3).

Frieda enthusiastically accepted my phrase 'put your whole self into it.' Taken literally, this sounds like the name of a method that many learners have profited from in recent years, called Total Physical Response (TPR).[1] In TPR, students spend much of their time getting up and doing things in response to instructions of increasing complexity: 'Go to the door,' or 'Take the pencil of the person sitting by the door, and give it to the boy in the green shirt,' for example.

For the most part, apparently, Frieda is not referring to a lot of physical activity. She seems to be talking more about full activation of her imagination, including imagined sights, imagined sounds, imagined feelings, imagined physical activity and so forth. The instructions given in TPR are *external* ways of ensuring that the students from a certain amount of the same kinds of *internal* imagery that Frieda generates for herself. Perhaps this is why TPR has been as successful as it has.

The activities that Frieda describes in this segment of her interview are largely noncommunicative (see 2.2.6). I would guess that communicative activities of various kinds, such as structured conversations (see 5.2.6) are effective because students cannot complete them without forming fairly full and complex mental imagery.

Working with the ideas

1. Where, in what Frieda said, did I find a basis for my phrase 'put your whole self in'?
2. Here are some sentences from actual language textbooks. Try to imagine situations in which you would use them:
   'How long have you been there?'
   'No, I've only read the sports section.'
   'It became darker and darker.'

6.1.3 Manufacturing one's own meanings

> ■ Two meanings of 'using' part of a language.
>
> ■ Finding an occasion, or imagining one.
>
> ■ Drills focused on either verbal or nonverbal imagery.
>
> ■ Tendency to assume that one's own way of learning is used by everyone.

'So you're really getting material both from the book and from whatever sources you can find standing around.'

'Mhm. You have to be very interested. You have to really want to communicate, because if you're just working with the material in the book, it's not enough. You have to be able to grasp each lesson step by step, and do it thoroughly and completely, and be able to *use* the material.'

'How do you mean?' I asked.

'For example, you're not given a chance within the class, or even within your own group, to use all the vocabulary and the structures. This is something you have to be able to work out for yourself in your own mind. You know, if you want to say, "My house is big," you have to be able to say, "My car is big" and so on. They give you a certain amount of drill in class, but you've got to drill yourself even more.'

'There's "using" in the sense of using it in a drill, and there's "using" in the sense of really having occasion to use it, or at least vividly imagining that you have an occasion to use it.'

'Mhm! You either find an occasion – you find people to talk to in Arabic – or you imagine to yourself that you do have the occasion to say it. If you don't have anybody to speak to, you can speak to yourself in a language.'

'Someone else might have looked at those same sentences in the same book, and said, "Well, these are just disjointed sentences. They're irrelevant." You kind of brought in and manufactured your own relevance, almost out of psychological whole cloth!'

'Uh huh! I think a lot of it is psychological! And it *is* relevant if you mix with native speakers of the language,' Frieda continued. 'And throughout my studies, I've always had friends from the Arab world. And if you can only say a few sentences to them, it's very nice, you know, in the course of an English conversation, even at a very elementary stage, if you can just throw in a sentence in Arabic. Or you can prepare ahead of time something very witty to say in Arabic.'

'And then set up a situation . . .'

'And then set up a situation where it would come in!'

Comments (c.f. 4.1.5)

When our interviewees have said '*You* do thus and so,' they have been describing their own experience and at the same time implying that it is true for everyone. Frieda does this much more than the others, however.

Frieda mentioned her need to 'use' all the vocabulary and structures, and then went on to talk about drills. In my reply, I pointed out that there are two ways of 'using' the words and grammar of a new language. In drilling, one works on the connections between the new element of the language and other words or grammatical patterns. In the other kind of 'use,' one concentrates on establishing and strengthening bonds between the linguistic element and the nonverbal imagery that fits it. Each of these requires its own kind of mental work.

Working with the ideas

1. In the comments on this segment, I mentioned two kinds of internal work that can contribute toward language mastery. Which of the two generally comes more naturally to you? Can you give examples?
2. Frieda's frequent use of 'you' suggests that she may assume that everyone is pretty much like her. In what ways are you aware of differences between your own language-learning style and the styles of other individuals? Can you give examples?

6.1.4 Shifting of attention during production

```
■ The eye–voice gap.

■ Smoothness as a goal in practice.

■ A 'Super-Monitor User.'
```

'I take it that memorizing is no great difficulty for you,' I said.

'No,' Frieda replied confidently. 'I don't enjoy it for itself, but if it has to be done, then it should be done.'

'Then by "perfecting" a text, you don't necessarily mean memorizing it?'

'No, no. Just reading it.'

'Just getting it so that you can do it smoothly.'

'Smoothly. Exactly! So the tone bears some resemblance to whatever is on the tape.'

'And having put all that work into a text, then the good results of that work are somehow available for other things you might want to do with the language later on?' I asked.

'Sure!' Frieda replied. 'It's a very good exercise. I still do it. No matter how advanced you think you are, there are always going to be tiny, tiny little things that you can brush up on.'

'And as you read, you listen to yourself?'

'Oh, yes! And you look ahead and prepare yourself for what you're going to have to say.'

'So there's a span of attention there, that runs maybe a syllable or two ahead, and also a syllable or two behind.'

'Oh, yes! And that takes work! But eventually you get to where you can look ahead and be reading at the same time, so that it sounds natural.'

Comments

Both Frieda and Ed tell us that they do a lot of reading aloud to themselves. Frieda, however, seems to do a great deal more conscious mental work as she reads than Ed does. She apparently has an unusual degree of ability to switch her attention rapidly among the sounds and the meanings and the grammatical features of the text. In so doing, she extends and strengthens her network of associations among all these aspects of the language. Then, as she speaks or writes, she is able to draw on this same network. She is what the originators of the Natural Approach would call a Super-Monitor User.

Working with the ideas

1. To what extent are you aware of giving attention to a number of different things as you read aloud?
2. As you read aloud in your native language, how many words or centimeters is your eye ahead of your voice?

6.1.5 A TECHNIQUE: Shifting attention while reading aloud
A technique from Frieda

This exercise may enable you to become more aware of your own shifting attention:

- Read aloud a paragraph (50–100 words) in your native language. What were you conscious of as you read?
- Read the same paragraph aloud a second time. Were you conscious of different things this time?
- Read it aloud a third time, giving special emphasis to the *m* and *n* sounds in it.
- Read it a fourth time trying to bring out the meaning for anyone who might be listening.

This exercise could, of course, be continued indefinitely, with attention on a different feature each time.

Try the same exercise in another language. Select some of your own points of focus: gender of nouns, endings of verbs or the like.

6.1.6 Paradigms

> - 'Just memorize it, write it out and pay attention to detail as you use it.'
>
> - The kinds of information that a paradigm contains, and the kinds of information it requires.
>
> - Working with a grammatical 'stockpile.'

We then went on to talk about how Frieda learned grammar. 'Well,' she began, 'I do have to be able to master the patterns that are presented to me in class. You have to be very, very confident with them. And after that, it's just drilling yourself.'

'Just drilling yourself in the sense of saying things over and over, or . . .?'

'I mean practicing composing sentences, and also doing the drills the teacher assigns. Learning grammar is actually a much simpler process than absorbing vocabulary or pronunciation. Some people say the grammatical structures are very hard, but it doesn't take that much time, for me at least, if you free yourself from the bonds of your own language. In standard Arabic,' she explained, 'mastering the grammatical patterns is just a question of practicing writing the drills, and practicing writing compositions with attention to all the details. It's less of an active process than the other aspects of learning.'

'In the sense that it requires less imagination, less energy?' I asked.

'Less imagination, yes, and less energy,' Frieda replied. 'It consists of things like committing to memory how to conjugate a verb.'

Frieda sounded casual about this. But memorizing paradigms had never been easy for me. 'In doing this, you . . .' I said, hoping that she would tell me how she did it.

'I memorize one verb and then apply it to the others,' she replied. 'It's just a question of practicing writing and speaking. It comes with time. At first it's just sheer memory work, dragging back into the depths of your mind asking, "Let's see! What's the past-tense feminine plural ending for this?" But some time later it becomes automatic.'

'Well,' I said to myself, 'at least it wasn't so easy for her in the beginning!' I also thought I was beginning to see how Frieda went at it. 'Listening to you describe all this, I think I'm getting a picture of what is happening,' I said. 'You have a kind of a stockpile of paradigmatic forms, and then you find occasions to use a pretty good sampling of these forms in conversation so as to make them stick.'

'Yes,' Frieda replied, 'it's the same idea. But there are far fewer forms in a paradigm than there are words in the vocabulary of Arabic. So the opportunities come up much more frequently. It's a shot in the dark to pick up a newspaper and expect to find in it a word that you've just studied. You have a much better chance of finding a particular combination of tense, person, number and so on.'

'But your way of going at it is to get the paradigms at least temporarily memorized, and then use the language. Then what you've stockpiled makes the actual use *easier*, but at the same time your use of it makes what you've stockpiled more *permanent*. Is that about it?'

'They definitely get more permanent!' Frieda replied.

'So you don't just stockpile the forms themselves,' I said. 'You also stockpile the skill of deriving other verbs from the ones you have memorized.'

'Mhm!'

Comments

A paradigm is a tabular presentation of all the forms of a particular noun or verb or other inflected word. It is really a special kind of 'rule' (see 5.2.4), or condensed summary of rules. Learning a paradigm is an extreme instance of stockpiling. For example, the paradigm of Old English *mann*, which meant 'person, man,' was relatively simple:

	Singular	**Plural**
Nominative	mann	menn
Genitive	mannes	manna
Dative	menn	mannum
Accusative	mann	menn
Instrumental	menn	mannum

In order to profit from a paradigm while speaking or writing, the learner must do the following:

■ Know the conditions that determine, at any given point in a sentence, which of the spaces in the paradigm (genitive singular, accusative plural, etc.) is called for.
■ Remember which form is found in which of the spaces in the paradigm.
■ Have access to all this knowledge within a tenth of a second or less.

No wonder paradigms are unpopular with most learners, and out of favor with most methodologists. Yet Frieda says that she makes use of them, and that the more often she uses them, the less time it takes. Perhaps she does. Some people do.

Working with the ideas

1. To what extent, if any, have you made use of paradigms? Would you recommend them to any type of learner? Why, or why not?
2. Which of the learners interviewed in the earlier chapters of this book do you think would find the use of paradigms most congenial? Why? Which of the learners would probably have the most trouble with them? Why?

6.2 Vocabulary

Frieda was also quite deliberate in building her vocabulary.

6.2.1 Vocabulary cards

> ■ **The power of personal relevance.**
>
> ■ **More tricks with vocabulary cards.**

'I gather that you've built up quite a good vocabulary,' I said. 'Can you tell us anything about how you've gone at that?'

'Well,' Frieda replied, 'with vocabulary, the easiest things to remember, of course, are the things that you want to say, the things you're going to have occasion to use, the things you've searched out for yourself. I asked someone one day how to say "vegetable grater," and I've never forgotten it.'

'A matter of personal relevance, urgency . . .?'

'Mhm. Personal relevance. Often things that are presented in textbooks, especially good textbooks, *are* things that are personally relevant. And if they're not, often you have to just sit down and commit them to memory, by writing them on little cards and memorizing them.'

'You've made a certain amount of use of ordinary word cards, then?'

'Yes. In the early stages, even if it's something that you want to say, you are going to have to write it down, and say it a few times to yourself before it comes naturally. I used to carry cards on the bus, put them up around the house – that kind of thing.'

'And what about that vegetable grater? What did you do about that word?'

'Oh, no, I didn't have to write that one down. This was in Tunisia. I wanted a grater very badly because I like to eat carrots, and I prefer them raw, and I prefer raw carrots grated rather than whole! They're more appealing that way!'

'So the word really fitted into your value system!'

'It very much fits in!' Frieda laughed.

Comments

Frieda's use of vocabulary cards appears to have been a little less sophisticated than Bert's (2.2.1). Presumably she wrote an Arabic word on one side, and one or more English equivalents on the other side. Even with simple cards like these, here are a few tricks that can make them more effective:

- If you are able to do a card easily, put it at the bottom of the deck. If you have to hesitate with it but then get it right, stick it into the middle of the deck. If you can't do it at all, put it back into the deck just a few cards from the top.
- Whenever else in the day you study the cards, go through them once just before you go to bed at night.
- Experiment to find out whether you get more benefit from reading the cards aloud or from just looking at them silently.
- Experiment also with different sizes of decks. For me, three decks of twenty-five cards each would work better than a single deck of seventy-five cards.

Working with the ideas

1. Have you had any experiences like Frieda's with the vegetable grater, where a particular word 'stuck' the first time you met it? What seems to contribute to this kind of learning?
2. Here is a list of ten English words that I did not know. With help from a dictionary if you need it, make word cards and study them as if they were foreign vocabulary:

hanse	guanine	scrim	scurf	bleb
decoct	decury	usance	wergild	agio

What variations of technique seemed most natural to you?

6.2.2 A TECHNIQUE: One way to use cards for vocabulary
A technique that Frieda might have liked

Here is a way of using word cards that does not involve just shuffling through the deck:

- Pick out ten cards that seem to be related in meaning.
- Concentrate on one card at a time, trying to form a nonverbal image for each one.
- Imagine a situation into which all ten of the words might fit.
- Collect the cards and, without looking, remove one or two of the cards. Put those cards where you cannot see them.
- Look at the other cards. The object is to give the words on the missing card or cards.

6.2.3 'Stockpiling' new items

> - **Foreseeing one's linguistic needs.**
> - **Practicing silently.**

'But not every word has that urgency when you first meet it,' I said. 'Yet you still go ahead and learn it?'

'If you think one day you *will* need it,' Frieda replied. 'And you usually do.'

'So some words you get on a "stockpiling" basis?'

'Yes, you stockpile them. But it's very important that you don't just stockpile them the way they are in the book,' Frieda warned. 'You have to *do* something with them. You can go out and buy a newspaper, or go to a movie, and some of these items you are stockpiling will show up in them. If that doesn't work, you can put the items into a sentence, just talking to yourself, about something that is going on. And in any of these ways, you can get reinforcement.'

'That is, while they're in the stockpile, you want to go out and find someplace in real life that will match up with them.'

'Exactly! And having matched them up, then that's what does it! If it's just in the stockpile, that's not enough, no matter how much you memorize it!'

'And when you did use word cards, how did you practice them?' I inquired. 'Silently? Aloud?'

'No,' Frieda replied, 'you practice them silently.'

'And what about the things from your stockpile that don't find partners in the outside world?'

'They're just lost!' she replied matter-of-factly. 'I just charge them up to profit and loss!'

'And how long could they stay in the stockpile before they get lost, do you think?'

'Oh, maybe a week or two. But I think it can't be emphasized enough that the study process is not detached from the real life that you're living! There are some people who can manage to study a language in a totally artificial environment, but they are very, very exceptional. That's not my style!'

Comments

This segment of Frieda's interview was the source of the 'stockpiling' metaphor that I have used frequently in comments on the other interviews. Although in the conversation with Frieda I was actually the one who used the word first, the enthusiastic way in which Frieda echoed it and continued to use it indicates that it fitted what she had been describing. I was interested in Frieda's apparent lack of concern over forgetting the items that didn't find partners in the real world.

Working with the ideas

1. Do you think it would have been better if Frieda had felt more concern at the prospect of losing a word that she was unable to tie in to real or realistic use? Which way would you tend to feel about the words in a new list?
2. How many hours or days do you think you would be able to keep a stockpiled word out of any meaningful context, and still have it available when the opportunity arose to use it?

6.2.4 FRED: Mnemonics

- Importance of understanding purposes and relationships.
- Using 'bizarre images.'
- Limitations on such techniques.

Fred was another interviewee about whose overall success I had no information. The language he was studying at the time was Japanese.

'If there's some kind of connection that can keep things going,' he said, 'I can remember things pretty well. For example, I can sit down and play a chess game with sixty moves, and when we're done, I can put the pieces back up and generally play through the game just from memory.'

'You've held on to all the moves,' I said.

'No, it's not that,' Fred replied. 'It's not that I memorized the moves themselves. But there was a logical sequence of why things were done the way they were, and that was what helped me to re-create the game as I went along.'

'And you feel that your work with language is similar?'

'Right. It's the same thing. If I can have a logical reason,' he explained, 'or even just create a story on why such-and-such is done in such-and-such a way, it helps me. I try to pin something else to the word – something that will help me get to it in a roundabout fashion.'

'Something that involves the word . . .'

'That involves the word in relation to other words in the language, if that's possible. But I can even tie a word to something in English. For instance, I had the hardest time remembering the word *tanoshi*, which means something like "pleasing." So finally I created a little idea of *tan-o-she*, that is, that a tan on women is pleasing.'

'And this little device stays with you? Stays with the word?' I asked.

'No. Eventually I'll be able to remember the word on its own, and then I can discard all that other stuff,' Fred replied. 'But it's really better to stay in the same language. Then there aren't so many links, or steps, or whatever you call them, that I have to go through. But these kinds of things definitely do work for me.'

'That's for remembering individual words. Do you have any techniques for remembering other kinds of things?' I asked.

'Well, in this course we have to memorize dialogs,' he said, 'and it generally works on the same principle. First I have to sit down and figure out exactly *why* people were saying *what* they were saying at each point . . .'

'Do you mean "why" in terms of their motivation, or "why" in terms of the grammatical structure, or . . .?'

'First of all, their motivations,' Fred replied.

Comments

Frieda told us that she sometimes 'stockpiles' words for later real use. Fred is also talking about stockpiling. Here he gives us examples of how he holds on to a set or a series of forms, whether those forms are chess moves or words or sentences in a dialog.

Fred's little *tan-o-she* device is called a 'mnemonic': an arbitrary association of something that is hard to recall with something that is easier to recall. Experimental psychologists call this one the 'bizarre images' technique, and have even tried to make it the basis of a 'Key-Word Method.' Over the years, several people have reported to me that they use mnemonics in their language study. Others, including some experts in language teaching, scoff at them. I don't know whether it is significant that not one of the seven highly successful learners whom I interviewed for this book had anything to say about mnemonics.[2] I do think, though, that it is important to remember that at best, stockpiling through mnemonics builds resources that have a very short shelf-life; as Dexter told us, if the words are not used in context very soon, they will evaporate and the time and energy that went into the mnemonics will have been wasted.

Working with the ideas

1. How is Fred's way of remembering isolated forms similar to Bob's? How is it different?
2. Have you ever had any success in using mnemonics for remembering people's names? For remembering phone numbers? For remembering things in foreign languages?

6.3 Pronunciation

Frieda went at pronunciation in very much the same way she tackled the other aspects of Arabic.

6.3.1 Producing sounds from printed descriptions

> ■ **Need for feeling comfortable with one point before going on to another.**

'And another important thing is to form a clear picture of what each sound that I'm going to make is like,' Frieda said. 'If I can get a written description of how a sound has to be produced, a sound that is not in English . . .'

'A description in words, or in the form of a facial diagram, or . . .?'

'In words is best. Telling me, for example, that this is supposed to be an alveolar *t*, or a dental *t*. This is very important to me. I read that and I study it. I started out with Arabic by practicing the sounds until I could . . .'

'Practicing out of a book?'

'Out of a book, and with the tape. Following the tape, and recording my imitations, and it was very important that with each step I had to be completely satisfied with my performance.'

'Before you tried to go on?'

'Yes.'

'And if someone had tried to force you to go on before you were satisfied, it would have been . . . troublesome.'

'It would have been *very* troublesome, I think! And I was fortunate that the course was paced in such a way that we were doing a few letters per day, learning how to write them.'

'So you were able to keep up.'

'Keep up and stay a little bit ahead. What was very important was mastering things. You have to feel that you really know what you're doing. At least for me, if I feel lost, there's no point in going on.'

'There's the mastery itself, so that you don't become *confused*,' I observed, 'and also a *feeling* of mastery, so that you don't get *disturbed*.'

'So that you don't get psyched out by the material itself!' Frieda answered.

'I wonder, is it primarily the cognitive mastery, primarily the feeling, so that you don't get psyched out, or both?'

'Oh, it's both. If you don't know the difference between one sound and another at a very early stage in the game, it's going to get worse as time goes on.'

'Confusion will compound itself.'

'Oh, yes!' Frieda replied emphatically.

Comments

Frieda says she produces new sounds by following printed recipes. I don't find this entirely incredible. (One time I found in a phonetics book a description of how to make an implosive *b*, a sound that I had never heard before. My first attempt was successful – too successful, as a matter of fact! I almost swallowed my Adam's apple.) But if what Frieda says here is true, this is an extreme example of producing language on the basis of rules (see 5.2.4).

Like Ed (see 5.1.6), Frieda is conscious of how her negative feelings can interfere with the cognitive process. This of course fits one of the points in the sequence I have outlined for the Natural Approach (see 1.1.4). But taking one point at a time and mastering it before going on to something else is 'learning' (see 1.1.2), and is very much in line with the principles of the CA-OB method (see 4.1.5).

Working with the ideas

1. I said to Frieda, 'so that you don't get disturbed.' What was there in the preceding conversation that led me to use this rather strong word?
2. Experiment with pronouncing the first sounds of the words *tie*, *pie*, *lie*, *sigh* and *nigh*. What happens to your tongue as you move from one of these sounds to another? (This is the sort of information that Frieda was getting from her phonetic descriptions.)

6.3.2 *Perfecting material before moving ahead*

> ■ **The place of conformity in language learning.**
>
> ■ **Listening to oneself on tape and off.**

'Pronunciation,' Frieda continued, 'is something that you have to be aware of almost all the time, until you get to the advanced stage.'

'You did say that you begin by listening to tapes and reading the printed descriptions of the sounds,' I recalled.

'Yes. You have to really, really know what you're doing with your tongue or whatever . . .'

'And when you look at a description that says "Constrict the pharynx," or whatever . . .'

'You've got to know how to do it instantly.'

'You yourself do know how to do that?' I asked. Very few people I know would understand that phonetic terminology.

'Oh, yes!'

'Did you teach it to yourself?'

'It's something the teacher usually helps you with, by repeating the sound, and you've read in your book that he is constricting his pharynx or whatever. It takes a little experimenting. It takes work with people, with teachers and with tapes, recording yourself and making sure that what you're producing is not way off the track.'

'To some extent monitoring yourself, then? Or depending mainly on the teacher?' I asked.

'No, you have to monitor yourself a lot. If you depend totally on the teacher, then once you step outside the classroom, you're going to be in hot water.' Frieda paused. 'Then after you get the sounds,' she went on, 'you have to deal with words. Some things come easy, and others you have to work and work and work. At the very elementary stage, when you can't read texts yet, it's just a matter of repeating certain words to yourself, over and over again. But as you go on, as you get more advanced in the language, you can take a text, and sit down by yourself, and read the text out loud, with attention to everything: with attention to meaning; with attention to the inflection of the sentences; and with special attention to the problem spots.'

'You're talking about reading the same text a number of times, shifting your attention from one thing to another?'

'Sure! You can do that, or you can do a number of texts. At the elementary and intermediate stages, it's basically a matter of working with one text, and what you're doing is, you're trying to perfect the text. And then when you speak, you have to be aware that you might mispronounce certain things, and try not to.'

'And you want to perfect the text because . . .'

'Because you know that if you do, you can move on to other things. If you can't pronounce that text, you're going to have real problems with doing anything else.'

Comments

Frieda again describes the way in which her attention shifts among various aspects of what she is doing (see 6.1.4). Her approach to pronunciation, one sound at a time, is in clear contrast to Ed, who told us he prefers to work with whole sentences at a time, and who finds the explanation of individual sounds not particularly helpful (see 5.1.5).

In this segment, Frieda gives a graphic description of the kind of internal mental activity that we called 'monitoring' (see 5.2.4). That is to say, she is carefully internalizing all of the teachers' 'do's and don'ts' so that they will be with her even when her teachers are not. In effect, she is developing her own 'linguistic conscience.' Most writers on language-use assume that this is merely a natural process which is necessary for full command of a language. Others, however, would say that she is becoming a willing victim of a tyrannical system of conformity, the purpose of which is to perpetuate the social power of the monolingual majority.[3]

Working with the ideas

1. In the comments for this segment, I mentioned two attitudes toward conformity with the norms of the monolingual speakers of a language. Which attitude do you agree with, or how would you reconcile the two?
2. Do you ever notice details of the pronunciation of other people? To what extent do you sometimes find yourself monitoring your own pronunciation?

6.3.3 The social significance of a foreign accent

- **Effects of refusing to conform.**
- **Influence of the learner's values and allegiances.**

'Have you had any experiences that would give you evidence of how authentic your accent may or may not be?' I asked.

'Oh, yeah, I have the experience of being taken for a native all the time! It's funny, because I don't look at all Middle Eastern, but it happens anyway. A few days ago some Lebanese took me for a Saudi. And that's quite extreme, because I don't look at all like a Saudi.'

'Now in Hebrew . . . You were in Hebrew classes only a short time, so I don't suppose you ever came close to sounding like a native speaker of that language.'

'That's an interesting question,' Frieda replied. 'In Hebrew you have the Ashkenazic accent of the European Jews, and the Sephardic accent of the Oriental Jews. I deliberately cultivated a Sephardic accent because I liked it.'

'And the teacher was probably an Ashkenazi!'

Frieda laughed. 'Exactly! And so the teacher said, "You have a very good Sephardic accent, but that's not what we want in this class!"'

'A bit of conflict right at the beginning,' I observed.

'Yes, and it was an ideological conflict, too! It was for ideological reasons that I cultivated a Sephardic accent. After all, Israel is a Middle-Eastern country, so why not speak the Middle-Eastern way?'

Comments

Some writers on language learning have distinguished between 'instrumental' and 'integrative' motivations for studying a foreign language.[4] 'Instrumental' motivations include the desire to receive a good mark in the course, or the desire to prepare for a better-paying job, or the need to read scholarly articles. 'Instrumental' motivations are the desire to become a member of the society that speaks the language, or at least to become more like them. Each of these two types of motivation can contribute in its own way to success with the language.

It sounds as though Frieda has either an integrative feeling toward one part of Hebrew-speaking society, or an anti-integrative feeling toward another part, or some combination of these. She shows this by her choice of who she wants to sound like and who she is unwilling to sound like. The human speech apparatus is capable of many more distinctions than are needed for mere intelligibility in any one language. All this reserve capacity is available for other purposes. Pronunciation is therefore a particularly handy medium for expressing such attitudes. We saw this also in the comments on 2.1.4.

In this connection, I know of at least three people who are virtuosos at speaking with various accents in their native language. All three have said that they don't 'do accents'; instead, they 'do people' they have known.

Working with the ideas

1. Why do we laugh when we listen to people intentionally speaking with other accents in our native language?
2. Hostile feelings toward a social group sometimes prevent other people from speaking with an accent that is characteristic of that group. But can you think of examples of times when you or someone else has used an accent as an expression of hostility toward its speakers?

6.3.4 *Wanting to sound like the other person*

■ **Learning in two ways at the same time.**

■ **Willingness to be laughed at.**

I wanted to find out a little more about Frieda's pronunciation of Arabic. 'You can sometimes pass for a native,' I said, 'but I don't believe that the printed descriptions of the sounds are that detailed – detailed enough to enable somebody to pass themself off . . . There's something . . .'

'No,' Frieda agreed, 'that's where the native speakers come in. And if you don't have somebody to speak with, you can listen to songs, watch movies, you can get tapes of theatrical productions . . .'

'But still,' I persisted, 'one sees people who go to theatrical productions and talk with native speakers for years, and they still come out sounding like Americans, and you apparently haven't.'

'Well,' she replied, 'you can't be content with just being understood. You have to have an active desire to sound like the lady you're talking with.'

'You didn't mind sounding like a non-American?'

'When I spoke? Oh, no! It didn't bother me at all! For fun, I would copy the way my roommate spoke English. It would drive her into a rage! Things like that. You have to be very interested in being able to copy what people say, how they say it, their mannerisms and all that.'

'And you seem to have some kind of knack for doing that.'

'I suppose. But in the meantime you mustn't mind being laughed at! People sometimes laugh, but they're laughing at your pronunciation, not at you. They're pleased with you for trying to learn the language.'

Comments

I had been skeptical for some time about Frieda's claim that her excellent pronunciation depended on the phonetic descriptions and diagrams in the textbook. What she says here about her desire to sound like the other person confirmed my skepticism. I can think of two possible interpretations:

- Frieda really did depend on the understanding she got from descriptions and diagrams for her first approximation of the sounds. Later, as she listened and practiced, she used her ear to further refine and polish them. This interpretation is consistent with the thinking behind the CA-OB method (see 4.1.5).
- The printed materials actually contributed little or nothing to Frieda's control of Arabic pronunciation. Their main value was that having them relieved her anxiety, and so allowed her mind to accept and work with the incoming sounds more readily. This interpretation is more consistent with the Natural Approach (see 1.1.4).

In any case, we have here an example of how two or more styles of learning can go on side by side. We should not assume that the kind of mental activity we are most conscious of is the only thing that is going on, or even the principal thing.

Working with the ideas

1. Which of the two interpretations of Frieda's pronunciation ability makes more sense to you? Why?

2. In what respects is Frieda reminiscent of Carla? In what respects are the two women quite different from each other?

6.3.5 Variant pronunciation of one's native language

```
■ Allegiances again.
```

There was one matter that had piqued my curiosity. In her pronunciation of the vowel sound in such words as *not*, Frieda consistently used the British form rather than the usual American one. The same was true for her pronunciation of *t* between vowels, as in *better*, and a few other matters. 'If you don't mind,' I said, 'I'd like to ask you about the way you speak English. I wouldn't say that you have an entirely American accent. Is this something you got from your family?'

'Yeah,' she replied, 'I speak exactly like my mother. And she speaks exactly like her mother.'

'But originally?' I asked. 'I've just come back from a conference where I heard a lot of English and Irish accents, and in some ways you sound much more like them than you sound like an American.'

'To an Englishman, I sound like an American!' Frieda laughed. 'Until people made me aware of it, I never was aware that I spoke any different from anybody else, but many, many people have said it to me!' Apparently I hadn't been imagining things!

'You actually grew up in New England, did you?' I asked.

'No! In Washington, DC!'

'And you went to a private school?'

'Yes, but not one where everybody spoke this way!'

'And you've maintained the way your mother speaks?'

'Yes! Any serious deviations from family pronunciation were looked down on! But it's not really family *pressure*.'

'It's just a very well-integrated family. A family that has pride in itself, and enjoys itself.'

'Mhm!' Frieda replied.

Comments

Just as we were at the end of the chapter on Carla, so we are faced here with a conundrum. We do not have enough information to explain why Frieda's pronunciation of English sounded non-American not only to me, but to some other listeners as well. (I found the same sort of mid-Atlantic accent in another interviewee, a young man who turned out to be from Amarillo!) Perhaps Frieda's pronunciation was a manifestation of some combination of integrative and nonintegrative motivations (see 6.3.3) toward various groups, including her immediate family.

Working with the ideas

1. Which of the points in Carroll's list (see 1.1.1) fit Frieda most obviously?
2. Which of the points in Omaggio's list (see 1.2.6) fit Frieda best? Are there any points in either list that do not seem to fit Frieda very well?
3. What seem to be Frieda's main sources of 'interactive,' as contrasted with mere 'linguistic' competence (see 3.1.2)?

6.4 Cultural considerations

I was interested in what Frieda had to say about the cultural and interpersonal side of her study of Arabic.

6.4.1 The etiquette of using a language with its speakers

> ■ **The need for assertiveness.**
>
> ■ **The value of patience.**
>
> ■ **Subordination of language to living.**

'This is a very active, aggressive way that you went at Arabic,' I observed, 'both with the textbook and with whatever opportunities you had outside. I don't mean aggressive in an undesirable way, of course, more what these days is called "assertive".'

'Mhm, you have to be aggressive!' Frieda agreed. 'As you say, not in an ugly sense, but in a way where you *want* to put things into the language!'

'You seem to really throw yourself into it. Maybe that's what it is,' I suggested.

'Mhm. That's what it is! You have to throw yourself into it! If you don't like the people and the culture, you're going to have an awfully hard time learning any language.'

'Your reactions to Arabs in general have been quite favorable, then.'

'Oh, yes. Of course, they've been different. I've had very, very good Arab friends, and that helps. I think one very important factor was that I lived with a girl from Kuwait for a year. She wanted to speak English around the apartment, but late at night, she'd get tired, and slip into Arabic very quickly.'

'You outwaited her!'

'I didn't have to outwait her. She'd be the one who came up with it. I was very careful not to force it on her, or on any native speaker. You know, they're in America, they want to practice their English on you. They can get very upset and feel threatened if you speak with them in Arabic.'

'Maybe they feel exploited?'

'Mhm. But, as you said, you can outwait people until they get tired of speaking English.'

'You're saying you have to be careful not to violate a respectful human-to-human relationship.'

'Mhm! And it's very important, because I've seen it happen a lot of times. People who want to practice the other person's language push too hard, and get very bad reactions from people, and they develop a real hate for the culture.'

'This means that it takes a lot of sensitivity and patience, and at the same time energy,' I commented. 'And energy and patience are two commodities that it's hard to manage at the same time!'

'Mhm!'

'The primary frame of reference is the human relationship. The language is only secondary.'

'That's right!'

Comments

Here Frieda brings into focus a problem that faces anyone who has social access to native speakers of the language she or he is learning. The problem is particularly acute, however, for a very able learner like Frieda – one who is good at 'stockpiling' material that must very quickly either be used or be lost. Some such learners are interested primarily in the personal satisfaction they can get from accumulating greater and greater command of the language. This attitude can lead to exploitation of the kindness of speakers of the language, and may quickly become offensive. Other learners see the new language principally as a means of relating with people. Taken by itself, this attitude can produce fluency in a variety of the language which is different from what native speakers use, and which may be difficult for them to follow. Frieda seems well aware of this dilemma. We saw a different aspect of it in 3.2.1.

Working with the ideas

1. Have you ever talked with learners of your native language who seemed more interested in the language than in what you were saying? Or have you even been such a learner?
2. Have you ever talked with learners of your language who were so interested in communicating with you that it was hard for you to follow what they were saying?

6.4.2 'Instrumental' and 'integrative' motivations

> ■ **Flexibility of the learner's self.**
>
> ■ **Perseverance.**
>
> ■ **Cultural openness.**

'Once I started Arabic, I never lost touch with it,' Frieda said. 'Once in a while I'd miss a lesson, but I'd always make it up to myself later. You have to feel that you owe it to yourself to learn it and to learn it well.'

'It's a real commitment. A very broad and at the same time very long-term commitment.'

'Mhm. It's broad. And it's long-term. It's not the sort of thing that you can confine to the classroom, and forget about between semesters.'

'Arabic is becoming a part of yourself. Or a part of yourself is becoming Arab!' I suggested.

'Yes, part of yourself is becoming Arab, not culturally, but linguistically. And even if you're not especially fond of certain aspects of *any* culture, you have to develop a respect for it, I think. Inside of yourself, you have to realize that they are people like the rest of us.'

'You don't have to enjoy them in order to respect them.'

'Exactly! But you have to realize that most people *can* be enjoyed, if you try to put aside some of your own prejudices.'

Comments

In 6.3.3, we distinguished between 'instrumental' and 'integrative' motivations for learning a new language. It is not entirely clear which of those terms is more applicable to what Frieda has told us here and in earlier segments. We will find that Gwen has something to say on the same question (see 7.2.3).

Working with the ideas

1. Which kind of motivation does Frieda seem to have toward the study of Arabic? What evidence can you find in what she says?
2. What can you guess about Frieda's motivation for the study of Hebrew?
3. What combinations of motivations can you find in your own study of other languages?
4. How would you rate Frieda in terms of the personality types mentioned in the comments on 2.2.1?
5. What further questions would you still like to ask Frieda?

6.5 Notes

1. The standard exposition of the Total Physical Response Method is by its originator, James J. Asher, under the title *Learning Another Language Through Actions* (Sky Oaks Publications, Los Gatos, California, 1982).
2. Irene Thompson has recently summarized the use of mnemonics for language study. This account appears as Chapter 4 of *Learner Strategies in Language Learning*, edited by Anita Wenden and Joan Rubin, and published in 1987 by Prentice Hall.
3. A particularly cogent statement of the view that language instruction all too often is a means for enforcing conformity and perpetuating the power of a ruling minority is found in Leo Loveday's *Sociolinguistics of Learning and Using a Non-native Language*, published by Pergamon in 1982.
4. 'Instrumental' and 'integrative' motivations in language learning are discussed in several books, including Doug Brown's *Principles* (Chapter 1, note 3) and my *Memory, Meaning and Method* (Chapter 3, note 2).

Chapter Seven

A Self-aware Learner

Gwen learning Japanese

Unlike the other six gifted learners, Gwen was a professional linguist and supervisor of language instruction. At the time of our interview, she had just been put in charge of Japanese instruction, and was also learning the language herself. Within the year that followed, she proved outstandingly successful in both respects.

7.1 Working on the mechanics of the language

7.1.1 From 'rules' to 'regularities' to 'resources'

> ■ Consciously introducing specific points of grammar into real conversations.
>
> ■ Exchanging practice sessions with speakers of another language.
>
> ■ The primacy of the social relationship.

Gwen began by telling me about an arrangement she had with a Japanese couple a little older than she was. She was spending half a day each weekend at their home, speaking Japanese with them part of the time, and English the rest of the time.

'Very frequently,' she began, 'I'll take a piece of grammar that I'm interested in, and consciously work on it.'

'Some structure, or some particular ending? That kind of thing?'

'Yes. For instance, last weekend I was working particularly on the passive. I know how to form it, but I still need time in order to actually do it. So last weekend I was paying particular attention to finding opportunities to throw it into the conversation.'

'You made a kind of game out of it,' I said.

'Yeah, it was like play. I was playing with the grammar, seeing how far I could go. Obviously there's a limit on how complex my sentences can get, and I do pay a price in fluency. And I sometimes pay a price in accuracy, too. But I find I don't really mind making mistakes in a situation like this. I feel very secure that our relationship is good, and that my friends don't seem to mind taking the time I need in order to get a sentence out.'

'And part of what gives zest to the game is the fact that you're pushing the edges of your linguistic security, and sometimes come out with things that aren't said in Japanese.'

'Oh, yes, quite frequently!' Gwen replied. 'Frequently I find things out that way. I sometimes have great triumphs, and sometimes of course I fall on my face – linguistically, that is. I don't mind that, because I know I'm secure with them socially. I know they're as interested in communicating with me as I am with them. Falling on my face linguistically doesn't mean falling on my face socially. That's the point.'

Comments
Gwen starts out with things she knows intellectually – the kind of things that in 5.2.4 was called a *rule*. We found this kind of thing also in 6.1.3 and 6.1.6. First, Gwen consciously applies the rule in order to construct a sentence in her head. But this cannot be just any sentence; it has to be one that fits in with whatever elements of meaning are present in her situation at the moment. When she produces the sentence, she forms a link between the rule she is using, on the one hand, and the meanings that are consistent with it on the other.

But Gwen doesn't stop with one sentence. While the rule is still fresh in her mind, she works it into the conversation several times. The sentences she forms with it are not identical. They do, however, illustrate some single principle – the principle described by the rule. Among them, therefore, these sentences give her practice with one of the *regularities* of Japanese. And if the conversation is interesting enough, she may also *remember* for a long time some of the actual wordings of the sentences. Gwen is doing what was described in 5.2.4 and later in Ed's account of his learning: she is generating regularities and remembered fragments to go along with her stock of rules.

Gwen is quite willing to make errors of language from time to time. She would be unwilling to offend her friends, however, or to be rejected by them. Her warm relationship with them allows her to keep those two possibilities separate in her mind. Keeping them separate frees her in two ways: she is able to maneuver the conversation more freely; and her mind absorbs the language of the conversation more fully. Whatever she absorbs will further develop and strengthen her network of resources for future speaking of Japanese. (After our interview was ended, Gwen told me that this interaction with the Japanese couple contrasted sharply with her early experience in another language. In that language, she felt that her teachers disliked her; not surprisingly, her progress was painful and slow.)

Working with the ideas

1. Gwen says she 'makes a game' of working some grammatical point into conversations with her friends. What socially useful skills are developed in the traditional games of hide-and-seek? I spy? Twenty questions?
2. What is the relationship between this 'game' of Gwen's and 'selective listening' (see 1.2.2)?

7.1.2 A TECHNIQUE: Working grammar into real conversation
A technique from Gwen

Gwen is able to participate in communicative activity while at the same time giving part of her attention to the form of what she is saying. She shares this ability with Frieda and some of the other successful learners we have come to know in this book.

1. Choose a daily, non-classroom activity that involves informal conversation in your native language or in a language in which you are comfortable. Try to work one of the following into what you say. (If your language is not English, select comparable features: features that are well-known but not very frequent.)

   'Be that as it may . . .'

   'Hardly had I . . . /Seldom have I . . . /Never have I . . .,' etc.

   Clauses that begin with *who* . . .: 'the people who came,' etc.
2. When you have had a little experience with this sort of thing in a language where you feel at home, try doing what Gwen did, working selected words or structures into apparently free exchanges.

7.1.3 The value of a bird's-eye view

- Doing without standard classroom activities.

- Structured conversation again.

- Shifting attention from the language to the learning process and back again.

'Overall, you're rather comfortable, then.'

'Yes,' Gwen replied, 'it's a very comfortable kind of thing. And yet I also need to go in with the intellectual awareness of what the patterns are. I'd say that's the role that standard classroom activities should play. Though I don't necessarily do them in an actual classroom. I very frequently do them on my own.'

'Reading grammatical descriptions or analyses? That kind of thing?'

'Reading, yes, or whatever,' Gwen replied. 'When I tried to learn in a regular classroom, in fact, I ran into a bit of conflict. It seemed to me I didn't need to do the dialogs and drills they wanted me to do in the class. I thought that was a waste of precious time!'

'They wanted you to do them just because that's what their other students had always done.'

'Yeah, but for my own mind, that's the kind of thing that, if I do it at all, I'll do on my own. I don't even find it particularly useful to memorize a dialog, or to do drills. I don't use tapes. I find that what I need is to get an intellectual awareness of something. I sometimes enjoy getting my own data and making my own analysis. On the other hand, if I'm in a hurry, I like having access to a published grammar of the language.'

'You don't like working in the dark.'

'Absolutely not!' Gwen answered. 'I remember how frustrated I was in high-school Spanish. We had one of those courses where you memorized dialogs, but you met the grammar only in piecemeal notes that followed them.'

'The grammatical information came just in little dribs and drabs.'

'Yes, and it was infuriating!' Gwen said. 'I wanted to see the whole system at once. The full paradigm of the verb, for instance. And that was when I was a sophomore in high school!'

'So one way or another, you get the necessary intellectual knowledge,' I said. 'But once you have that intellectual understanding, in a fairly abstract sense, you're able to work directly from that to the kind of situation that you had last weekend. A situation where, while engaged in the give and take of real communication, you are able to draw on what you have stored intellectually . . .'

'Mhm,' Gwen replied.

'To draw on it, and put it into sentences that are at the same time a part of the communication, and are also little linguistic trial balloons.'

'Well, I suppose they are almost drills,' Gwen said thoughtfully. 'I mean, I *am* setting up repetitive situations. But they aren't mechanical.'

'They're drill-like activities which are at the same time completely a part of something else that's going on besides language drills.'

'Yes! Yes, I'm doing two things at once.'

Comments

Like Derek, Ed and Frieda, but unlike Carla, Gwen seems to be able to focus simultaneously on *what* she is saying and *how* she is saying it. Or perhaps it would be more accurate to say that she is able to shift her focus very rapidly from one to the other and back again.

When she comments, 'Well, I suppose they are almost drills,' Gwen is reinforcing the distinction between the external form of most drills, and their essential purpose. (We talked about this distinction in 5.2.6).

Some methods go to great lengths to protect students from having to do drills, and from having to contemplate tables of verb forms. Yet Derek insisted on getting the whole picture even if he had to paint it himself. Ed talked about the 'frustration' he felt when he was not allowed to drill on a new point of grammar. Now Gwen uses 'infuriating,' a word with even heavier emotional loading, about the experience of being denied a look at a full paradigm. Perhaps their exceptional ability to make use of resources that daunt some other people is what makes Ed and Gwen into 'gifted' language learners. Or perhaps some of the methods to which I have just referred have been 'throwing the baby out with the bathwater.'

Working with the ideas

1. In what ways, if any, is Derek's or Ed's strategy here more congenial to you than Gwen's is? In what ways is hers closer to what you might do?
2. What aspects of your own language study would you be most likely to describe in emotionally loaded terms?

7.1.4 GRETA: The need for a 'power base'

- A social inhibition against informal conversation with bilinguals.

- Once more, the influence of perceived social reactions to one's efforts.

Greta was studying a relatively difficult language. I do not know anything about her overall aptitude or her eventual success.

'I studied some German before we went to Salzburg,' Greta began, 'but I'm afraid I didn't use much of it while I was there.'

'You didn't have occasion to?' I asked.

'Well, it was mostly at social gatherings,' she replied. 'And there, so many people knew a certain amount of English. For me, I need motivation . . .'

'And being with people who could speak English didn't . . .'

'Didn't give me that motivation, no. Whereas in France we made some French friends who didn't speak English, so if we were going to a dinner or something, and I knew what the topic was going to be, I'd try to learn a few words that I thought would be useful, and then I'd work them into the conversation.'

'The motivation you're talking about then consisted in . . .'

'Two things, really. One is that I don't like to learn things, even people's names, unless I feel I'm really going to have a need for them later on.'

'It just isn't worth it otherwise.'

'That's right. And the other is that I'm sensitive if somebody looks at me as if to say, "You said it wrong," or "That's not really what you would say to me." Even in the class I'm in right now, it's the same way. I'm sensitive to the fact that much of the time we're saying things in a way which from the teachers' point of view is "all right for now," but which isn't really the way things are said. Even though I don't know much of the language, I can still pick up the fact that something isn't . . . right.'

'You're very cautious.'

'Right! I'm better at looking and reading and just producing short sentences,' Greta replied. 'I like to concentrate on what I'm supposed to be concentrating on. Then later, as our vocabulary builds up, *then* put more words in and start saying more.'

'You'd rather start off with a very small amount of stuff, and build up a kind of little power base, a very small but very solid power base, and then move out from that as you can . . .'

'Exactly! I know it may be better to take chances now and then, but as it is, if I'm to be motivated to speak, I need someone who can't either understand or speak English.'

'And that would make it all right to speak!'

'That would make it all right, because whatever I would say would be, you know, better than nothing . . .'

Comments

Greta obviously lacks Gwen's aptitude and experience, and most of all she lacks Gwen's self-confidence. I suspect that in this regard most of us would identify more with Greta than with Gwen. Yet both women are alike in that they consciously and deliberately establish 'power bases' for themselves and then move outward. This much is reminiscent of the CA-OB method (see 4.1.5). Both also illustrate the principle that one's ability to speak is limited or expanded according to the reactions that one sees (or thinks one sees) in the people with whom one is talking.

Working with the ideas

1. What is the nature of Gwen's 'power base'?
2. Compared with Carla, what weaknesses and what strengths do you find in Greta?
3. If Greta came to you asking for advice on how to learn languages more easily, what advice would you give her?

7.1.5 The value of semi-attentive listening

> ■ **A further example of 'acquisition' by adults.**
>
> ■ **'Osmosis.'**
>
> ■ **An experience with Swedish.**

'And another thing about having the intellectual understanding of the language and how it works,' Gwen went on. 'It goes beyond just making up my own sentences. It also helps me be aware of what is happening in what I hear.'

'But you're after all a professional – a highly skilled learner,' I remarked.

'No question about that,' Gwen conceded. 'But I don't always learn by these skilled-learner types of thing. I do a lot of my learning by a kind of osmosis.'

'Just soaking it up without direct effort. Just being around people who are really using the language.'

'That's right!' she replied. 'Even if you don't understand it all. But pretty soon things will begin to sink in, or at least they do for me if I'm around the language long enough.'

'And on your weekends with your Japanese friends,' I asked, 'do they give you some of this, or do they pretty much stay within your limits?'

'No, they're pretty good about speaking at my limits and pushing me. They're always a little beyond my limits. That's good. And sometimes they just talk to each other.'

'Then you hear some real Japanese.'

'Then I hear some real Japanese. I guess the thing that's frustrating to me then is that I know I'm still not ready for that, and I still need what you might call "sheltered Japanese."'

'Frustration at seeing how far you've come and how far you've pushed the borders back, and yet realizing . . .'

'Realizing that I still can't handle the undiluted language.'

Comments

Gwen says that 'even if you don't understand the language you are hearing around you, pretty soon it will sink in.' I had this experience once when, for the better part of a week, I sat in the back of the room sketching while a group of language teachers discussed professional matters in Swedish. Between classes, I also tried to read day-old newspapers in Swedish. Fortunately, I was able to draw on my general knowledge of the subject matter, and also on previous exposure to German and Old English. In the beginning I was able to catch only isolated words out of the conversation. As time went on, however, I found myself understanding phrases and even occasional whole sentences. It was great fun!

When Gwen uses her professional skills at analyzing and organizing language data, she is 'learning' in the special sense of 1.1.2. What she here calls 'learning by osmosis' is really 'acquisition,' akin to what happens when a child is gaining control of its first language. For this purpose, people who can speak near one's limits but a bit above them are an ideal resource (see 3.1.5).

Gwen combines the intellectual power of a Derek or an Ed with the acquisitional ability of an Ann or a Carla. I think it is safe to say that she has learned more languages, to a higher degree of personal proficiency, than all of the others combined.

Working with the ideas

1. How would you compare the 'frustration' that Gwen describes here with the 'frustration' Ed complained of in 5.2.6?
2. In her use of 'osmosis,' which of the other gifted learners does Gwen most closely resemble? Why?

7.2 Other matters

7.2.1 Reading for pleasure

- Maintaining a 'running inventory.'

- Reading silently for pleasure vs reading aloud as recitation.

- Again, a feeling of things slipping into place.

- We learn relationships *among* items, as well as the items themselves.

'One thing I like to do,' Gwen said, 'is to read novels in foreign languages.'

'Primarily for their literary value, or because it gives you access to native speakers?' I asked.

'For two reasons. One is the depth that they give to my contacts with live speakers – and depth of understanding of the language too, of course. I also read them for fun. When I was in Thailand, I used to get people to recommend things they thought I'd enjoy.'

'Enjoyment was more important that literary quality.'

'Oh, definitely! And now in Japanese, one of the things I do by myself is read, because it's a kind of exposure to the language – an exposure that I have control over. I don't need somebody else for it. I don't have to fit it to someone else's schedule.'

'Novels again?'

'No, no. At this point I'm still reading stuff that's prepared for learners. But it's fun. It really is.'

'Reading silently?' I asked, thinking of Ed.

'Both, actually,' Gwen answered. 'Reading aloud is something I've always hated. As a kid I was terrible, even in English. I used to get nervous. I felt I was being judged for my performance. But I find I actually enjoy reading aloud in Japanese!'

'You hated it in English, but you now enjoy it in Japanese?'

'Yes. I think it's because I don't feel it's a performance kind of thing. My reaction to reading aloud in English was a little like my reaction to typing. I'm a terrible typist. When I type, as soon as I make my first mistake, I tighten up and it starts a downward spiral.'

'But in Japanese it's more like a game?'

'In a sense, yeah, but not a competitive kind of game. It's a game I can play with myself.'

'Like a jigsaw puzzle?'

'More like that, yes. The reward you get when you feel a piece of the puzzle plopping into place!'

Comments

Like Ed, Gwen reads aloud. I would guess that the benefits she gets from this activity are something like the ones described in 5.1.1. Unlike Ed, however, Gwen does not appear to depend on it.

When she talks of 'a piece of the puzzle,' and when she says she feels that something is 'plopping into place,' Gwen echoes what Derek said (see 4.1.2). It sounds almost as though she and Derek and Ed are maintaining in their heads a kind of running inventory. This inventory includes more than their grammatical resources. It also includes the relationships *among* those resources.

Working with the ideas

1. How does Gwen's antipathy to reading aloud differ from Carla's (see 3.2.2)?
2. Are there any kinds of activity outside of language study in which you sometimes find yourself in a downward spiral like the one Gwen describes?

7.2.2 Developing pronunciation through 'acquisition'

I raised the question of pronunciation.

'I don't make a big deal of pronunciation,' Gwen replied. 'I'll try to establish a certain amount of accuracy from the beginning, but I don't worry very much about it.'

'You don't try to perfect it.'

'No, I don't. Because I found that if I can get the exposure, it takes care of itself. I think that's borne out by my results with both Cambodian and Thai.'

'The way people respond to you?'

'Yes. I think it depends partly on subtle things like intonation. When I'm with Cambodians, after ten or fifteen minutes they begin to feel there's something funny going on. They'll say things like "How long have you been in this country?" When I first heard that, I was taken aback. But now I realize they just mean they thought I was Cambodian, maybe Eurasian, and had been out of Cambodia long enough so that I talked a little funny.'

Comments

With her extensive training in phonetics, Gwen could have developed her intellectual understanding of how the sounds of a new language are made. She appears not to have done this. This 'acquisitional' approach to pronunciation contrasts with her more academic practice of first seeking intellectual understanding of a new sound through printed descriptions (see 6.3.1) or visual observation (see 5.1.5).

Working with the ideas

1. Gwen, Derek and Ed seem to share the experience of being taken for native speakers, or at least for non-American speakers of languages they have learned. How does Gwen's approach to pronunciation compare with Derek's or Ed's?
2. How does Gwen's approach to pronunciation compare with Bert's?

7.2.3 Identifying with others while preserving one's own identity

> ■ 'Integrative' motivation(?)
>
> ■ **Participating while maintaining perspective.**

Gwen then went on to describe a very interesting angle on pronunciation. 'I think the reason I do get the pronunciation eventually,' she said, 'is that I have a kind of feeling of wanting to be like the people in the country, and the people I'm associating with. I really do. It was like that with the Cambodians, for instance, though of course I fully recognized I would never be one. But still, to the extent that I could, I wanted to assimilate to that social group.'

'And presumably this has been true for a rather long succession of peoples over your language-learning career,' I remarked. 'A very consistent urge to associate with . . .'

'To *identify* with them, without in any sense denying my identity as an American. I don't see any real contradiction. I don't think being open to other people is incompatible with being a good American. I recognize that I'm a product of my culture and never will be anything but an American, but at the same time I can get a very deep understanding of whatever culture I'm relating to, and enjoy, in a sense, putting on another self.'

'Almost like a part in a play. Yet this is not play in the sense that you're making fun of anybody or looking down on anybody.'

'Oh, no! It's a very respectful thing.'

'Respectful, and also a very deeply fulfilling kind of thing to be able to go on being basically an American, and yet to be able to relate with them in a way so that they can begin to react almost as if you were one of them.'

'Yes, with the understanding that I'm not going to be completely one of them. But to the extent that people can sort of let their hair down just a little bit with me, it is a very rewarding sort of thing.'

'It sounds as though you had almost developed a separate self for each culture.'

'No, I don't have any sense of separate selves! I really don't! It's a very natural sort of transition when I stop speaking English and go into Indonesian or Thai. It's not like having a closetful of selves hanging up on hangers and taking one down and putting it on. I'm still me. I've still got the same thoughts and the same feelings. But I tend to react in a different way when I'm in a different framework.'

'It's more like different sides of yourself, and you turn to each person the side of yourself that is appropriate.'

'Yes. More like a faceted crystal. Yes. But in the beginning stages, it's very convenient to be able to be just a plain American.'

'You can use that status in order to establish yourself as a learner and set out on the kind of path that you typically follow – a path that will eventually lead . . .'

'Into greater assimilation. Yes.'

Comments

How can an adult develop excellent pronunciation in a foreign language? There are two unsubstantiated beliefs on this subject. One is that pronunciation consists of a combination of muscular habits, and that these habits need to be built up one at a time through systematic practice. The other belief is that anyone with normal speech apparatus *will – though not immediately –* sound like whomever he or she really wants to sound like, regardless of systematic practice. In this view, a person who consciously wants to speak without an accent, but who unconsciously doesn't like to sound 'foreign,' will always have more or less of an accent. On the other hand, a person who has never studied phonetics, but who wants to fit in with the new culture, will speak with little or no accent. Gwen clearly fits better with this second view than with the first. In spite of what Frieda said, her pronunciation also seemed to support this motivational interpretation (see 6.3.4, 6.3.5).

Working with the ideas

1. How do you understand Gwen's distinction between 'separate selves,' and separate 'facets' of her single self?
2. How would you describe her motivation with regard to pronunciation? Is this a motivation that you could easily share?
3. In what respects was Gwen building her 'interactive competence' and not just her 'linguistic competence' (see 3.1.2)?
4. What questions would you still like to ask Gwen?

Chapter Eight

Summary

8.1 What worked for these learners

8.1.1 An overall pattern

The learners we have met in this book often differ markedly with regard to what they consider to be 'natural,' and what they prefer to do or not to do. They differ also with regard to the kinds of data they seem to hold onto best. Ann depends on her ear and is quite content to repeat things before she has seen them in writing; Frieda would probably have failed Hebrew if she had not found a way to see the printed lessons ahead of time. Ed, Eugene and some of the others want to understand the structure of things before they practice them; Carla is ready to practice immediately, but has trouble with the requirement to deal with grammar. Gwen dislikes drills and Carla was defeated by them, but Bert, Derek, Ed and Frieda place high value on this kind of relatively mechanical activity. Ann is excellent at mimicry, while Bert didn't even try it. Ann simply cannot learn words out of context; Bob, Bert and Dexter are good at it. And so on. Hardly a clear model for an aspiring language student who wants to profit from their example![1]

But a learner should also be cautious about accepting guidance from us specialists in language pedagogy. Too often, we fail to resist the human urge to 'construct an entire method on one brilliant insight' – to 'latch onto one key idea and follow it long and far,' as Karl Diller once put it.[2] Somebody notices that much can be gained, at least with certain learners, by practicing sentences aloud before seeing them, or by picking up grammar without formally studying it, or by understanding grammar before practicing it, or by maintaining a tranquil atmosphere in class, or in some other way. These insights all too easily lead to the conclusion that reading should be minimized, or that grammar study should be done away with, or that it should be given first place, or that teacher-generated challenges are always bad or the like. In one of A. A. Milne's verses, the discovery that 'marmalade is tasty if it's very thickly spread' brought about an immediate movement to delete butter from the king's breakfast menu altogether.

Nevertheless, I think I see emerging out of all these contrasts and contradictions an overall pattern. Each of the learners I interviewed illustrates some parts of that pattern; none of them illustrates the whole pattern; yet none of them seems to me really to contradict it. In describing that pattern, I will be using three common words in slightly uncommon ways. The three words are 'image,' 'nonverbal' and 'verbal.'

- One's *image* of something is not just a visual 'picture in the mind.' It is one's whole basis for action in relation to that something. One's image of one's kitchen enables one to find things in the kitchen, or to direct others to find things in it, or to draw a sketch of it, or to decide that it needs to be redecorated.
- *Nonverbal* imagery includes the kinds of data that come in through the traditional 'five senses': color, distance, size, sound, texture, flavor and all the rest. But it also includes emotions and purposes, and such things as duration and frequency and remoteness in time. Nonverbal imagery provides the meanings that we put into our words and infer from the words of others.
- Our *verbal* imagery is the basis we have for pronouncing sounds and words, and for putting words together into larger combinations. As I am using the term, we have a verbal 'image' of how to pronounce the word for a young wool-bearing animal that says 'baa,' and we have a verbal image of how to form relative clauses or negative questions. To the extent that our verbal imagery is like everyone else's, we speak 'correctly' and 'idiomatically.' To the extent that it is unlike the verbal imagery of established speakers, we 'make errors.' And to the extent that our verbal imagery for a particular word is incomplete, we 'can't quite come out with the word' at all.

8.1.2 Elements in the pattern

'Language'
First of all, then, 'language': this is a book about the 'learning' of 'languages.' When we think of a 'language,' we tend to think of sounds and letters, of words and phrases, of sentences and paragraphs and poems and sales pitches. But these by themselves are only the audible or visible physical *form* of a language – the *verbal* side of using it. By themselves they would be worthless. They become valuable only as they convey meanings: only as they enable us to tell other people what we have seen, or to describe skills that we have and want to teach to them, or to convey what we want them to do or think or feel. These are *meanings* – the *nonverbal* side of using language.

Connecting the nonverbal with the verbal
Simply stated, then, on the technical level, language learning consists in forming a set of appropriate mental connections between the verbal and the nonverbal. Insofar as we have formed these connections, we can get the right meanings from the sounds or scribbles of other people. We saw this process at work in all our learners, most dramatically as Ann eavesdropped on the Scandinavian teachers (see 1.2.1). But we can also produce sounds and scribbles that will convey our own meanings to others.

When language learning has been successful, this process seems easy and natural: all we are aware of is that we just 'say what seems right' (see 3.1.1).

Nonverbal communication

Yet not all communication involves words. Perhaps Ann really did communicate with animals at the zoo and with human babies (see 1.1.5), both she and they using and responding to subtle cues in posture and gesture and tone of voice. If this was indeed genuine wordless communication, it was a striking example of it. Less sensational, but much closer to the center of what goes on in everyday language study, was the nonverbal communication from teachers and classmates as felt by Carla (see 3.2.3) and Frieda (see 6.1.1, 6.3.4) and Gwen (see 7.1.1). Some readers of Carla's interview have even concluded that hostile nonverbal communication from others was the principal source of Carla's difficulties in the German class. I have certainly seen cases of the opposite, where supportive, encouraging nonverbal communication has helped people to speak better. In my comments on 3.2.3, I mentioned research which also supports this principle.

Mental images as mediators

So far, what I have said is merely a restatement of general wisdom in the field of language learning. In fact, though, we do not connect our 'verbal' material – our words and phrases – *directly* to external realities. Rather, we connect that material to *mental images*. In 8.1.1, I tried to clarify how I am using that term in this summary. Contrary to what we commonly suppose, mental images are not little copies of external reality. They usually *begin* with material drawn from what has come in from outside through our eyes, our ears, our skin and all the rest. But then the mind takes those external data, fills in around them from past experience and so produces the final images – the final meanings – that we are aware of. This active, creative nature of understanding is illustrated both by what Ann got right as she listened to the Swahili conversation *and* by what she got wrong (see 1.2.4).[3]

Images as bases for action

Once again, as in 8.1.1, I would like to emphasize that I am using the expression 'mental image' here in a very special way. In everyday language this phrase often refers to some kind of mainly visual picture in the mind. Most people have such experiences, although for some the pictures are much more vivid than for others. But we also ask each other questions like, 'What's your image of Iowa?' or 'What's your image of the ideal presidential candidate?' The answers to these questions commonly include references to sounds, feelings and many other sensations in addition to the purely visual. As I would like to use the term, then, one's 'mental image' of a thing or of an event or of a person or of a problem is whatever *basis one has for possible action in relation to* that thing, event or whatever.[4] And the word 'action' here does not necessarily mean 'going and doing something' in the usual sense. It also includes describing and talking about and even reacting emotionally.

The variety of elements in nonverbal images
This image – this 'basis for action' – is the product of a whole *network* of relevant associations, and these associations involve data of many kinds. Certainly people talk about what they have seen in a purely *visual* sense. But Frieda's image of the Sephardis and the Ashkenazis – her networks of what her past experiences had led her to connect with them – contained *social* elements (see 6.3.3). Similarly, Carla's image of 'using German' contained *social* elements: her enjoyment of friends (see 3.1.5) and her embarrassment at being 'laughed at' (see 3.2.1), for example. The same is true of Greta's reluctance to use a foreign language when the people she was with might prefer that she use English (see 7.1.4). *Social* elements also run throughout the interview with Gwen. On the other hand, Frieda's 'vegetable-grater' image (see 6.2.1) was full of *utilitarian* purposes. For Bob (see 2.2.3), the *'feeling'* component was particularly important.

'Verbal images'
We could say that the two things we connect as we use language are verbal *symbols* and nonverbal mental *images*. But I would like to go a step beyond this. After all, coming up with the words we need, or forming a negative imperative sentence, or pronouncing the vowels right, or using appropriate intonation – all of these are actions too. The 'bases for' these actions must also be produced, in part, from information stored in the mind. In this sense, as I said in 8.1.1, I like to talk about *'verbal images'*: the mental resources that enable us to come up with the spoken and written linguistic symbols and patterns of symbols that we need when we need them. 'Nonverbal images,' on the other hand, are what generate the meanings: the feelings, the pictures, the sounds and all the rest.

The variety of elements in verbal images
Like nonverbal images also, verbal images result from a combination of associations in many modalities. Most obvious, of course, we *hear* what others say and we also listen to ourselves in order to be sure that we are saying what we meant to say. And of course we *see* words on paper (or blind people *touch* them) in order to read. Ed reminded us (see 5.1.1) that as we speak, we must also *feel* what our tongue and lips are doing. (Try speaking when you've had a local anesthetic that interferes with this!) *Emotions* and *purposes* make up two other very important modalities in nonverbal imagery.

Other modalities
But verbal images draw on other modalities as well. I have already said that an image is created from a network that includes information in all these modalities. So it often happens that data from one modality will trigger something in a quite different modality. Most obvious is the relationship between letters (which we see) and sounds (which we hear), and this is one place where Carla seems to have had some trouble (see 3.2.2). Performing actions while we talk about them provides *kinesthetic* links with nonverbal material. Some people seem to get value from

associating the *auditory* part of verbal imagery with the *kinesthetic* experience of writing things out (see Eugene 5.1.2) or of saying them aloud (see 5.1.1). But just the sound of a particular language being spoken may trigger all sorts of powerful *emotions*. (This, I think, is a major component in the working of 'integrative motivation' (see 6.4.2).) The same is true of listening to various dialects even of our native language. And for Ann, as for many of us, there were *geographical* associations tied to certain pronunciations of English (see 1.1.2).

Individual differences in using various modalities
People differ greatly, however, with regard to the strength or frequency of the various kinds of associations from which they create their images. Most obviously, few of us experience the clear *visual* results that Aileen got from a combination of *auditory* and *emotional* sources (see 1.1.6). We also differ as to the kinds of data that we retain best and rely on most. Thus Eugene says he could not do without writing, Bert depends on the kinesthetic resources that come through using his voice and jaw and tongue in repetitive drills (see 2.1.2, 2.1.3) and Frieda claims she relies on printed descriptions (see 6.3.1).

Images are produced, not retrieved
One thing about all images, whether verbal or nonverbal, is that we do not actually store them in our minds as fixed, stable images. That is to say, we do not have fixed, stable records of how to pronounce *schism*, or of the way to the post office or of the postal employee who usually sells us our stamps. Rather, our minds *produce* these images – these 'bases for action' – fresh for every occasion, out of the countless associations that we have formed between those things and other things that we have met along with them. These associations among an item, and other items associated with it, and still other items associated with those other items, commonly form a complex network. If one's network of associations related to a particular person (or a particular word or grammatical construction) does not change much from one occasion to another, then one's image of that person (or word or construction) will apparently remain constant. But insofar as the relevant network does change, the image that it produces will be modified accordingly. (The literature of cognitive science provides repeated support for this statement.[5])

Parallel images for 'the same thing'
In the normal course of living and using language, we are commonly aware of only one such 'basis' for each of the acts we want to undertake, or for each thing we want to say. Sometimes, however, our minds generate competing 'bases for action.' The two come out side-by-side (or in very close succession), and we are able to compare them. For example, when Ed talked about monitoring his own speech, he was saying that he had derived one 'basis for action' from what seemed natural to him, and another from the rules and sets of inflected forms that he had memorized in class (see 5.3.2). Ed then compared the two sets of *verbal* images and made a choice. That was what Frieda was doing as she 'monitored,' too (see 6.3.2). As a student in

an Audio-Lingual Method French course I found that generating and comparing parallel verbal images – one set from rules and reasoning, the other more or less echoically – was a valuable way of doing repetitious drills. Much of Carla's difficulty came from her inability to generate a parallel set of verbal images from learned rules, in order to check on her spontaneous output (see 3.1.5). On the other hand, when Bert paraphrased sentences and stories in Chinese (see 2.2.6), what he and his teacher were comparing were two sets of *nonverbal* images: those that came from the original sentences and those that came from Bert's version.

Three simultaneous processes

Combining nonverbal material. So learning a language consists of *three processes that go on more or less simultaneously*. In one of these processes, we match up *nonverbal* images with other *nonverbal* images to form larger nonverbal imagery. An example is Bert's gradual piecing together of the elements of Chinese culture (see 2.1.3). This was certainly one of the benefits that Gwen got from her recreational reading, too (see 7.2.1).

Combining verbal material. In a second process, we piece together *verbal* images with other *verbal* images. These were the components of Derek's charts (see 4.1.2), and they were undoubtedly what Gwen and Derek felt 'plopping' or 'slipping into place' from time to time (see 7.2.1, 4.1.2). Frieda's verb paradigms are clusters of verbal images (see 6.1.6), and her dredging through 'the depths of her mind' in order to come up with a needed form constitutes exploration of these clusters.

Matching verbal and nonverbal material. In the third of these processes, we match up *nonverbal* images with *verbal* images. This is the process that comes most readily to our conscious attention when we think about how we use language, but it depends on the other two. It is illustrated in nearly every section of every interview in this book. Fred's system of attaching pictures and English translations to Japanese words is only the most overt example. We find the near-absence of this third process as Bert repeated unconnected sentences hour after hour and week after week, with little or no consciousness of their meanings (see 2.1.1). Morton's first student of Spanish (see 2.2.5) is a more extreme example of the same thing.

'Learning' and 'acquisition' in this pattern

All normal human beings have innate equipment for learning language from the largely unorganized flow of speech and other activities that sweep past them from birth (see 1.1.4). This equipment enables us to distinguish nonverbal from verbal material, and to sort all this material out. Then we match the pieces up. By doing so, we build networks that become a never-ending source of images – of 'bases for action.' For an adult like Carla, most of this 'acquisition' (see 1.1.2) is unconscious – a matter of what Gwen called 'osmosis' (see 7.1.5). Chuck also seemed to do a lot of 'acquiring' (see 3.1.6). For adults such as Bert, Derek, Ed, Frieda and Gwen, however, conscious 'learning' seems to make an important contribution to the building of networks. In either case, the process is complete when the resulting verbal and nonverbal images enable us to deal smoothly and effectively with other speakers of the language.

Moderate speed of input is helpful for 'acquisition'
The unconscious 'acquisitional' kind of activity seems to go forward most easily when the 'torrent' of verbal and nonverbal data is replaced by a steady but moderate flow. Carla's boyfriend and his family spoke to her in German which was authentic, but which was also at or near her level (see 3.1.5). Gwen's friends did the same thing for her in Japanese, and she for them in English (see 7.1.5). Carla in Moscow (3.1.5) and Chuck in Denmark (3.1.6) found out that an unmoderated flow of language makes learning or acquiring less efficient, though not impossible.

Nonverbal images without verbal counterparts, and vice versa
In everyday experience, we constantly form nonverbal images with little or no verbal imagery to go with them. It is also possible to form verbal images with little or no nonverbal imagery, though some people are much better at this than others are. Morton's student (2.2.5), Derek's charts (4.1.1), Gwen's paradigms (7.1.3) and Frieda's phonetic recipes (6.3.1) all illustrate this possibility. So do the various references to 'stockpiling,' and the affirmations of the value of drills (see 2.1.3, 4.1.7, 5.2.5).

Ultimately, nonverbal and verbal material must come together in the learner's mind
If nonverbal and verbal images are to be joined in a way that will lead to language mastery they must be together in the learner's mind. This commonly takes place when the external stimuli that trigger their production, both nonverbal and verbal, are coming in at the same time. This was true for Carla with her friends in Germany (3.1.5) and in Brazil (3.2.1), as well as for Ann at the Indian hotel (1.1.4) and Chuck in Denmark (3.1.6). And of course it is a regular feature of many teaching methods including the Direct Method, Total Physical Response, the Natural Approach, the Silent Way, and various communicative techniques that are widely used today.

Deliberate manipulation of imagery resources
But nonverbal and verbal images may also be juxtaposed by bringing them out of memory, with more or less activity of the imagination. This was what Derek was doing when he created his 'brother's' vagaries (see 4.2.2), and it is the basis for his maxim about learning to want to say what you can say (see 4.2.3). Here also is Frieda talking to herself (see 6.1.2) and Barney (see 2.2.6) planning what he would like to ask the man he had met briefly. Perhaps those of us who profit from memorizing texts and from performing mechanical drills get value from those activities because we are a bit more adept than other people at constructing meanings – 'nonverbal images' – for a fixed string of words that have been given to us outside the context of normal communication.

'Stockpiling'
Nonverbal images accompanied by little or no verbal imagery may last a long time in memory. Similarly, verbal images accompanied by little or no nonverbal imagery may be retrieved from memory, as Frieda, Fred and Gwen showed us (see 6.2.3, 6.2.4, 7.1.1, 7.1.3). But the shelf-life of unaccompanied verbal images is much shorter than for many nonverbal images (Dexter, see 4.2.4, 6.2.4), though Bert claimed that some of his verbal images were still available after six months (see 2.1.2). The best way – perhaps the only way – to move verbal materials from the 'stockpile' to permanence is through putting them to use. This is what Dexter meant by attaching words to experience rather than to their positions on the page. This is what Elsa's friend had to do immediately with the lists of German words that he had memorized (see 5.2.1). What Bert had 'swimming around in his head' were not words, but sentence patterns waiting to be attached to experience. This may also have been the value that Ed found in structured conversation (see 5.2.6).

Using material from the 'stockpile'
Last but not least, we have repeatedly seen that learners have more success when they participate actively in their own learning. They can do this in at least three ways. One is by creating their own meanings (their own nonverbal mental images) for words, or words for meanings. Examples of this kind of participation were cited in some of the preceding paragraphs. Derek speaks of 'the difference between receiving something and making it' (see 4.2.3). Ed says very much the same thing (see 5.2.4), and talks about mentally 'performing a sentence along with the person who is speaking' (see 5.1.3). Daniel's student and Dora were certainly doing the same sort of thing (see 4.2.5).

Controlling one's own learning
Two other ways of participating in one's own learning are by planning what one is going to undertake, and by designing one's tools. Remember Carla with her Japanese-speaking friend at work (see 3.1.3). In her social conversations with the Japanese couple, Gwen had a very clear idea of her linguistic goals (see 7.1.1). Similarly Frieda had definite mental lists of words and verb inflections that she wanted to find situations for (see 6.2.3). Ann devised her own phonetic transcription even though one was already provided in the textbook (see 1.1.3).

Acceptance of responsibility
A third way of participation in learning is to accept much of the responsibility for how things turn out. Derek is most explicit about this principle (see 4.1.1), but it is implied in much that the other learners did as well.

8.2 Conceptual gaps in this book

8.2.1 Some concepts that have been included

In the comments on the interviews, we met a number of concepts that are often discussed by specialists in the study of languages. Some of the most conspicuous have been the 'learning–acquisition' contrast; various kinds of motivation and various meanings for the word 'communicative'; the role of affect or emotion; and the phenomenon of 'monitoring.' We also saw more than one side of certain disputed issues in the field, including the value of learning rules, and the advisability of doing large amounts of mechanical practice.

8.2.2 Some concepts that have been omitted

There are of course several other concepts and issues that are of equal interest to theorists. For example, I have said little or nothing about the relationships that appear to exist between personality factors such as introversion/extroversion or field dependence/independence, and style of learning or overall success with languages.[6] Another fascinating body of research that casts light on the learning and use of language has to do with the process of trying to recover a word that is 'just on the tip of my tongue.'[7] These matters simply did not come up in the interviews, however, and I have omitted reference to them. This book is not intended as a comprehensive treatment of second-language acquisition. I have set out only to introduce and comment on certain individual learners. Perhaps by understanding a bit about these people, readers will come to understand themselves better as learners.

8.2.3 'Strategies'

Much has been written recently about the 'strategies' employed by people who are learning languages. In the opening chapter of an influential book on that subject, Anita Wenden[8] uses the expression 'learner strategies' to refer to three kinds of things (p.6):

- What people *do* in order to learn a new language.
- How they *manage* or *self-direct* these efforts.
- What they *know* about *which aspects* of their learning.

In this sense, the interviews in Chapters 1–7 contain evidence about a wide range of 'strategies.' But Wenden (p.7) also points out that other writers have used different terms for much these same three kinds of things, and that 'strategy' has itself been used in a variety of ways. For this reason, and because the term is not yet a part of the public vocabulary, I have largely refrained from using it in this book.

8.3 What I myself would do with a new language

Some readers of the manuscript of this book have asked me how I myself would go at the study of a new language. Am I, they wonder, more like Ann, or Derek, or perhaps like Gwen? My first reaction to this question was that those who posed it were really asking, 'Which of the interviewees did it best? What, after all this documenting of diversity, do *you* think is the *right* answer?' If that was indeed the intent of the question, then I ought to refuse to answer it. My second reaction, however, is that the question as asked is a perfectly fair one, which I should not evade.

Ultimately, of course, the answer is that I am not sure how I would approach a new language. It would depend partly on the structure of the language, and partly on the social and geographical setting in which I was studying. Yet there are a few points that seem fairly clear to me.

1. Lots of listening before speaking
I would like to hear a lot of the language before I tried to say anything in it. I might listen to the radio, watch TV or go to the movies as Chuck did, or just sit and listen to real people. Some of my listening would be inattentive, the way it was in Swedish (see 7.1.5), but at other times I would concentrate my attention on one aspect of the sound after another, the way Frieda sometimes did. Occasionally, even at the beginning, I would try to guess what was being said. Ann was especially good at this. (I have found that for some unknown reason I can frequently get *meanings* better if I consciously try to focus on each *sound* – each vowel and each consonant – as it goes by.) From time to time, I would also see how much I could get from examining a whole newspaper – the technique I mentioned in connection with 1.2.3.

2. Tie language to some coherent reality
When I began to say things, *I would prefer that what I said be true to some coherent reality*, even if only a 'reality' that I had made up in my own mind. Here I would be very much like Derek. I would be less concerned with how communicative my sentences were (how much new information they conveyed to other people), or even with how (on what levels) they were communicative. Bert's paraphrasing practice would therefore appeal to me.

3. Produce true sentences in families
I would like, at least part of the time, to be able to *produce these true sentences in families that were partially like one another*: *That is a bench. That is a porch. Those are armchairs.* Or *I'm drawing a picture. I drew two pictures this morning. Did you draw any pictures yesterday?* Structured conversations of the kind that Ed was talking about are a good vehicle for producing families of true sentences.

4. Understand what is going on linguistically
Whenever I ran into unexpected complications in moving from one sentence to

another in these families, *I'd like to understand fairly soon what was going on*. On the other hand, I'd rather my teacher not seize on my request for a brief explanation of one particular thing that *I* don't know, and turn it into an occasion for telling me everything *she or he* thinks I ought to know about the general topic. I seem to be like Derek and Ed in this respect.

5. Verify understanding by trying it out

Once I thought I understood a new complication, I'd like to have a chance *to verify (and if necessary, to modify) my understanding of it by making or hearing new families of sentences*. Structured conversations again! This sounds like Ed, and also like Gwen. And like Frieda or Dexter, I find that things stay with me better after I have put them into a meaningful exchange with someone else.

6. Do some mechanical practice

Having clarified my understanding of the new point in this way, I would like to have (in fact, I would probably insist on having) a chance to do *a fair amount of purely mechanical practice*, something like the technique with the cuisenaire rods that I described in 4.1.3. Bert, Ed, Derek and Frieda are all with me here! I would even do a certain amount of memorization, because memorization is easy for me and because I have frequently been able to use in conversation various adaptations of things I had learned by heart.

7. Practice aloud

I would certainly want to make use of written materials, but in the early stages I would try for retention of new words and structures *mainly through practicing out loud*, much as Ed did. Like Ann's, my memory seems to be more aural and kinesthetic than visual. I might use the 'shadowing' technique of Daniel's student and Dora (see 4.2.5). Even more, however, I would develop my pronunciation by just listening to and repeating after tapes. In this respect I am different from Ed.

8. Repeatedly listen to and produce the same material with a native speaker

Another of my favorite techniques is *to tell something to a speaker of the language, and have that person tell the same thing back to me in correct, natural form*. I then tell the same thing again, bearing in mind the way in which I have just heard it. This cycle can repeat itself two or three times. It easily (for me, at least) leads not only to greater correctness, but also to memorization, and as I said in (6), I am one of those people who can draw on memorized material while I am speaking. An essential feature of this technique is that the text we are swapping back and forth originates with me, so that I control the content and do not have to worry about generating nonverbal images to match what is in someone else's mind. That was one benefit of Derek's decision to invent a brother for himself. I think Gwen would like this little device, too.

9. Find the right people to talk with
In the above technique, and for conversation practice in general, I would seek out the right kind of person. Like Carla and Gwen, I am aware of *how much better I do with people who seem to enjoy talking with me*. Like them also, I would prefer someone who had the knack of speaking to me in language that was authentic, but that was only a little beyond my level.

10. Guide my own learning
Like Gwen, I prefer *to guide my own learning as much as I can*, rather than just sitting back and being taught.

11. Try for interaction, not just language practice
Last, but by no means least, I would try to arrange matters so that whatever competence I developed would be not only 'linguistic' but also *'interactive'* (see 3.1.2).

What I have outlined here is pretty close to what I would do. Readers may find that some parts of my list fit them, too, but I am sure they will find other parts of it quite unsuitable. The only list that will really fit readers will be the ones they make up themselves. I hope that along with the interviews in Chapters 1–7, this personal list of mine may have stimulated readers' imaginations and added to their insight. Then they will be better able to make their own choices.

8.4 What this means to me as a teacher

1. Be sure that both verbal and nonverbal material are actively present in students' minds at the same time
I have also been asked how the interviews have affected my own view of teaching. My answers to this question will, I am sure, continue to grow and change with the passing of years. Right now, my first thought is that in order for the Language Acquisition Device (1.1.2, 1.1.4) to operate, both verbal and corresponding nonverbal resources – what I have called 'images' (8.1.2) – must be present, fresh and active in the mind of the learner. I think this has been true in one way or another for all seven of the successful learners. It is not enough that those resources be present in the mind of the teacher. It is not even enough that the students have the necessary information from which, given time and motivation, they *would be able* to construct these images for themselves.

2. Remember that students differ in their handling of various aspects of input
The interviews have provided numerous and sometimes dramatic illustrations of the fact that learners differ as to the kinds of data – visual, auditory, social, grammatical, and so on – which they respond to most readily, retain most dependably and around which they construct the verbal and nonverbal images they need. I must be on the lookout for surprising weak spots in the best of learners, and

for unexpected strengths in their more ordinary sisters and brothers. As a lesson-planner, therefore, I need to provide many kinds of resources on which students may draw. Some will pick'up one kind of information out of the same lesson from which others will pick up other kinds.

3. Let students 'stockpile' material, but keep track of what is in the stockpile
With Bert, Derek, Ed and Frieda in mind, I will not be afraid to encourage students to stockpile verbal information and skills through systematic exercises or through other kinds of practice where the focus is on linguistic form. I will however consider that kind of effort wasted unless the new verbal resources are very soon incorporated into language that is tied to students' purposes and emotions and not just to other words, or just to some pedestrian pedantic truth.

4. Use explanations, but do not rely on them
With students like Frieda or Gwen, who seem to need or crave explanations and organized descriptions of how the language works, I will not hesitate to provide that kind of help. On the other hand, I will not place much reliance on it. And for Carla's sake I will not force those concepts on students who seem unable to handle them.

5. Arrange for students to say things they have some reason for wanting to say
Remembering Derek's maxim, I will endeavor to arrange for my students to very much want to say things they are able to say. To some extent I can do this by how I design my materials and plan my lessons. But Carla and Frieda and Gwen will not let me forget that *wanting* to say things is going to depend partly on how my students feel towards the people they are talking with (their classmates and me), as well as how they think the rest of us feel towards them.

6. Beware of building a system of teaching around one type of learner
Finally, I ask myself what would happen if a Gwen on the basis of outstanding personal accomplishments in language learning, or a Derek because of some brilliant intellectual formulation, or an Ann through force of personality, or one of the others in some other way, suddenly came into a position to set a new trend in language-teaching methodology. What would such a methodology be like? Would Bert have learners repeating and paraphrasing with little or no translation or explanation? Would Carla insist that people go out and associate with friendly native speakers who knew how to limit their language for foreigners? Would Ed have everyone reading aloud, or would Derek set a generation of students to constructing their own charts of noun and verb inflections? Surely any such methods would be partially successful, but each would also contain the seeds of defeat for some students.

These are not idle questions, either, for exactly this kind of thing has happened time and again in the history of language teaching. The social prestige of literary scholars lay behind the Grammar–Translation method, and the practical achievements of the anthropological linguists during World War II produced a methodology built around their strengths. One after another, successive innovators have cast and recast 'the learner' in their own image. Even as an individual teacher, may be tempted to act as if all students really *should* be like me at my best, or perhaps like my most illustrious alumni. So I will remember Diller's warning (see 8.1.1) about the temptation to take one experience or one small set of principles and push that experience or that set of principles too 'long and far.' Whenever someone offers me a new technique or asks me to embrace yet another approach, I will ask myself, 'How would this fit ——?' and into the blank I will substitute first Ann, then Bert, then Carla and Derek and Ed and Frieda and Gwen.

8.5 Notes

1. 'How-to' guides for language study appear from time to time. I have already mentioned Moulton, and Larson and Smalley. Another is Paul Pimsleur's *How to Learn a Foreign Language*, published in 1980 by Heinle and Heinle.

   Those who would like to inform themselves *about* language teaching may enjoy Wenden and Rubin's book (note 4, Chapter 6). It contains chapters by many leaders in the field, including Andrew Cohen's account of his observations of individual learners. A landmark study of the subject is *The Good Language Learner*, by N. Naiman, M. Fröhlich, H. H. Stern and A. Todesco, published in 1978 by the Ontario Institute for Studies in Education.

2. The Karl Diller quote is from *The Language Teaching Controversy* (Newbury House, 1978), pp. 148 and 150.

3. The active, creative nature of memory comes out clearly in J. D. Bransford's book *Human Cognition* (Wadsworth, 1979). Although this book is not about the learning of languages, its extraordinarily clear development of basic concepts make it a pleasure to read and use. Two other very readable books for the educated layperson are Ulric Neisser's *Memory Observed* and Donald A. Norman's *Learning and Memory*, both published in 1982 by Freeman.

4. This meaning for 'image' was first suggested to me by B. R. Bugelski's article on 'Learning and imagery', which appeared in the *Journal of Mental Imagery* in 1982, vol. 6.2.

5. The concept of 'network' appears in many studies in memory, including John R. Anderson's discussion of 'Spreading activation' in *Tutorials in Learning and Memory*, which he edited with Stephen Kosslyn (Freeman, 1984). It also appears near the beginning of David Rumelhart's chapter on 'Schemata: The building blocks of cognition,' in *Theoretical Issues in Reading Comprehension*, edited by R. Spiro, B. Bruce and W. Brewer (Erlbaum, 1980). Neither of these books is as accessible as the Bransford, Neisser and Norman books, however (note 3, above).

6. A readable survey of some of the factors that go into 'cognitive style' is Dayle Davidson Hartnett's chapter 'Cognitive style and second language learning' in *Beyond Basics*, edited by Marianne Celce-Murcia (Newbury House, 1985). Another such study, 'Effects of sex differences, career choice, and psychological type on adult language learning strategies,' was published by Madeline Ehrman and Rebecca Oxford in the *Modern Language Journal* in 1989, vol. 73.1.

7. These phenomena are described in S. Glucksberg and J. H. Danks, *Experimental*

Psycholinguistics (Erlbaum, 1975) and in H. H. Clark and E. V. Clark, *Psychology and Language* (Harcourt Brace Jovanovich, 1977). A more recent exploration of the tip-of-the-tongue phenomenon is J. Reason and D. Lucas in *Everyday Memory, Actions and Absent-mindedness*, edited by J. E. Harris and P. E. Morris (Academic Press, 1984).

8. See Chapter 1 of *Learner Strategies in Language Learning*, edited by Anita Wenden and Joan Rubin (Prentice Hall International, 1987).

9. A very practical and well-organised book on this subject is *Language Learning Strategies: What every teacher should know*, by Rebecca L. Oxford. (Newbury House, 1990).

Index

accent, foreign, 28, 70, 76, 82, 84, 119
accuracy, 22, 54, 100
acquisition, 4, 8, 30, 40–44, 48, 50f, 53, 59f, 87, 101, 133, 136, 143
active nature of understanding, 140
active participation, importance of, 9, 19
AILEEN, 10, 142
Anderson, John R. 151
animals, apparent communication with, 9
ANN, 30, 41, 43, 54, 56, 60, 63, 74, 75, 121, 139, 140, 142, 143, 144, 145, 147, 148
aptitude, 2, 48, 53
Arabic, 103
Asher, James J., 105, 126
attention, focus of, 76, 83, 84, 108, 118, 130, 147
attitude of interlocutor, importance of, 11
attitude of learner, 19, 29, 85
Audio-Lingualism, 22, 25, 38, 67, 73, 97, 103
auditory memory, 83
auditory verbal images, 83
aural learning, 104, 148
authentic materials, use of, 5, 26, 35, 47, 147

BARNEY, 38, 144
'begin with vocabulary, or with structure?' 87
BEN, 36
BERT, 51, 58, 60, 67, 86, 94, 112, 142, 143, 144, 145, 147, 148
bizarre imagery, 115
BOB, 141
bottom-to-top (*see* top-to-bottom)
Bransford, J. D., 151

Brooks, N., 39
Brown, H. Douglas, 20, 39, 126
Brumfit, C. J., 39
Bugelski, B. R., 151
'build from strength!', 88, 104, 132
'burn the patterns into the brain!' 26
Burt, M., 20, 102

Cambodian, 135
CA-OB (Cognitive Audio-Oral Bilingual) method, 64, 73, 81, 97, 101, 104, 117, 121
Cards (*see* word cards)
CARLA, 64, 73, 92, 124, 130, 139, 140, 141, 142, 143, 144, 145, 149
Carroll, John, 2, 19f, 32, 56, 66, 122
Celce-Murcia, Marianne, 151
challenges, 44
charts/tables of forms, 65, 144
Chinese, 21
CHUCK, 143, 144, 147
Clark, E., 152
Clark, H. H., 152
cognition, necessity of, 81, 89, 115, 130, 148
Cohen, Andrew, 151
communications, 38, 71, 100, 105, 130
  nonverbal, 140
  with animals, 140
communicative, 37f, 106, 147
comparing mental images, 47, 91, 143
competence, 149
competing images, 143
concentration, 77, 83, 85, 97f
confidence, 53
conformity, role of, 119
connecting verbal with nonverbal, 139

image as 'basis for action', 140
  competition among, 143
  derived from networks, 142
imaginary brother (*see* Derek)
imagination, in producing nonverbal
      imagery, 38, 71, 77, 105, 145
informal and formal study, relation
      between, 48
instrumental motivation, 28, 87, 120
integrative motivation, 28, 120, 121, 122,
      123, 125, 136, 142
interaction among modalities, 142
interaction with native speakers, 47, 49,
      50, 56, 69, 72, 74, 82, 105, 107,
      127, 144, 149 (*see also* etiquette)
interactive competence, 43, 72, 97, 123,
      137, 149
intonation and rhythm, 69f, 80, 83f, 108
intuition, 7

Japanese, 44, 114, 127
Jespersen, Otto, 56
Johnson, K., 39
juxtaposing verbal and nonverbal images,
      144

'Key-Word Method', 115
kinesthetic component of meaning, 34,
      142, 148
Korean, 54, 79
Krashen, S. D., 20, 102

Language Acquisition Device (LAD), 4, 7
language learning or acquisition: view of
      the Natural Approach, 7
language, what it is, 139
Larsen-Freeman, Diane, 39
Larson, Donald N., 102
Latin, 31, 80
learner attitude toward material, 85
learning, 30, 40, 50, 53, 64, 87, 101, 133
  (in contrast to acquiring), 4, 38, 41ff,
      51, 53, 59f, 87, 101
Loveday, Leo, 126
Lucas, D., 151

mass media, 48
'master one thing at a time!', 106, 117, 118
matching verbal and nonverbal, 105, 110,
      114, 143

meaning, importance of, 81, 84
meanings of language, 25, 36
memorization of texts, 23, 29, 34, 42, 44,
      60, 103, 108, 115, 130, 148
  of vocabulary, 32, 60, 75, 80, 112, 115
  through writing, 81
mental files and indexes, 64
mental imagery, 38, 140
mimicry, 4
  in Ed's sense, 97
mnemonic devices, 115
modalities in images, 141
  interaction among, 142
monitoring, 47, 91f, 94, 99, 102, 108, 118,
      143
monolingual requirement in class, 24
Moody, R., 39
Morton, F. Rand, 36, 39, 143f
Moskowitz, G., 102
motivation for achievement, 125
motivation, instrumental (*see*
      instrumental)
motivation, integrative (*see* integrative)
Moulton, William G., 5, 20, 39
multimodality (*see* modalities)
Myers–Briggs Type-Indicator 32, 56, 125

Naiman, N., 151
Natural Approach, 8, 54, 64, 73, 101, 108,
      121
natural, what seems to be, 18, 21
Neisser, Ulric, 151
networks of associations, 94, 97, 108, 128,
      141ff, 151
Nida, Eugene, 2, 20
nonhuman communication, 140
nonverbal communication, 10, 140
nonverbal images, 6, 17, 143, 145
  connections among, 27
Norman, Donald A., 151
Norwegian, 1

Omaggio Hadley, Alice, 19f, 32, 56, 60,
      66, 122
originating one's own texts, 45
osmosis, 133, 143
own mental work, importance of doing, 6,
      45, 60, 62, 65, 73, 91, 94, 130, 145,
      149
Oxford, Rebecca, 39, 151